D0897102

Marathon

© The Archaeological Society at Athens
22 Panepistimiou Ave, 106 72 Athens, Greece
Fax (01) 3644996

ISSN 1105-7785
ISBN 960-7036-57-3

English translation: Alexandra Doumas
Editing: Kate Ninou
Layout: Ilektra Andreadi

THE ARCHAEOLOGICAL SOCIETY AT ATHENS LIBRARY NO 155

| 7 | ANCIENT SITES AND MUSEUMS IN GREECE | 7 |

BASIL PETRAKOS

HON. EPHOR OF ANTIQUITIES FOR ATTICA

Marathon

ATHENS 1996

Contents

MARATHON AND THE TETRAPOLIS   1

THE PLAIN OF MARATHON   3

THE BATTLE OF MARATHON   8

  The conflict   8

  The betrayal   15

  Herodotus' account   16

  The Tumulus of the Athenians   18

  The excavation of the Tumulus   22

  The grave of the Persians   24

  The trophy   26

  The announcement of the victory   30

  Ex-votos at Delphi   32

  Ex-votos at Athens and Plataea   34

  Legends and cults related to the battle   35

  The significance of the battle for posterity   37

  Miltiades   39

  Aeschylus the Marathon-fighter   44

  The polemarch Callimachus   47

TOPOGRAPHY OF MARATHON   50

  The Heracleion   50

  The Makaria spring   52

  Plasi   55

  Tsepi   58

  Vrana   59

  The tholos tomb   63

The Classical tumulus   65

The sanctuary of Athena   67

Mikro Helos - Nisi   68

The sanctuary of the Egyptian Gods   74

The balneum   81

The Cave of Pan   85

The Pythion at Oinoe   90

MYTHOLOGY OF MARATHON   97

HERODES ATTICUS AT MARATHON   100

   His life   100

   His estate   101

   His *ex-votos*   106

THE MARATHON MUSEUM   119

   Gallery I   119

   Gallery II   123

   Gallery III   135

   Gallery IV   150

   Gallery V   166

   Courtyard   179

Abbreviations   183

Notes   184

Publications of the pottery and the minor arts in the
Marathon Museum   194

Sources of the photographs   197

Marathon and the Tetrapolis

The large village nowadays known as Marathon did not occupy the same site in antiquity. Its territory then was divided among four demes, *Marathon, Oinoe, Trikorynthos* and *Probalinthos*. The first three belonged to the Aiantis tribe and the fourth to the Pandionis. All four comprised a local union, the *Tetrapolis*. Although the boundaries of these demes have not been established, the district of each can be accurately determined on the basis of inscriptions and literary evidence. Sporadic building remains, inscriptions, cemeteries, the foundations of houses or farmsteads have survived from these demes. Their sanctuaries and political centre, that is the *agora*, have not been discovered as yet. The demes of the Tetrapolis were four neighbouring villages in the wider area of present-day Marathon, that extends from Nea Makri to Oinoe (Noinoi) and Kato Souli.

In the descriptions of the sites or monuments the demes of the Tetrapolis to which they belonged are mentioned. When precise determination is not possible they are attributed in general to Marathon, the largest and best known deme.

There are various explanations of the provenance of the name Marathon. According to Dikaiarchos[1] it was given by *Marathos* from Arkadia, who campaigned with the Dioscuri in

Attica. Pausanias[2] speaks of an eponymous hero, *Marathon*. In reality the name derives from the herb *marathos* (fennel), which to this day grows wild all over the Marathon plain. Indeed an ancient comic poet, Hermippos[3] (425 BC), alludes to the relationship between the plant and the place, saying of the battle in 490 BC: 'ὥστε Μαραθῶνος τὸ λοιπὸν ἐπ᾽ ἀγαθῷ μεμνημένοι/πάντες ἐμβάλλουσιν ἀεὶ μάραθον ἐς τὰς ἁλμάδας' (as a pious reminder forever of Marathon, all put fennel in the salty olives).

The Plain of Marathon

T he fertile, coastal plain of Marathon is bounded to the 1
West by the foothills of Mount Penteli, Agrieliki, Kotroni
—the ancient form of which has been lost because a large helicopter pad has been constructed recently on its summit— and
Stavrokoraki. Principal features of the topography of the plain
are the two marshes, Mikro Helos (Small Marsh) or Brexiza's,
north of the American base, and Megalo Helos (Large Marsh),
which extends north and northwest of the beach at Schoinia.
The great battle of 490 BC took place between the two
marshes, in the region of the Tumulus. The Athenians were on
the west side, with Agrieliki behind them, while the Persians
were ranged on the actual plain, east of the Tumulus, surrounded by the sea, the Large Marsh and Stavrokoraki.

Continuous cultivation and ploughing in the Marathon
area, the silting up of the plain and the drastic changes in recent years due to the transformation of large tracts of arable
land into unplanned settlements, have inhibited the uncovering
of remains of ancient monuments probably preserved there.
Moreover, we should bear in mind that the upper structure of
many of the buildings —public, private and sacred— in the
four demes was in the main constructed of mud bricks, which
have been destroyed without trace. Thus the only testimony of

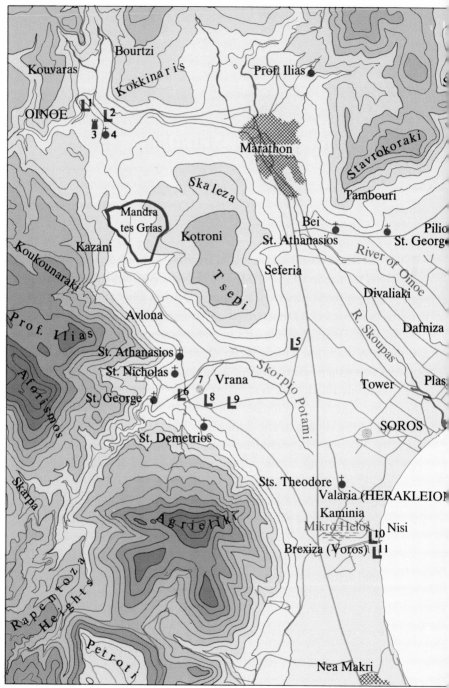

Fig. 1. Map of the region of Marathon.

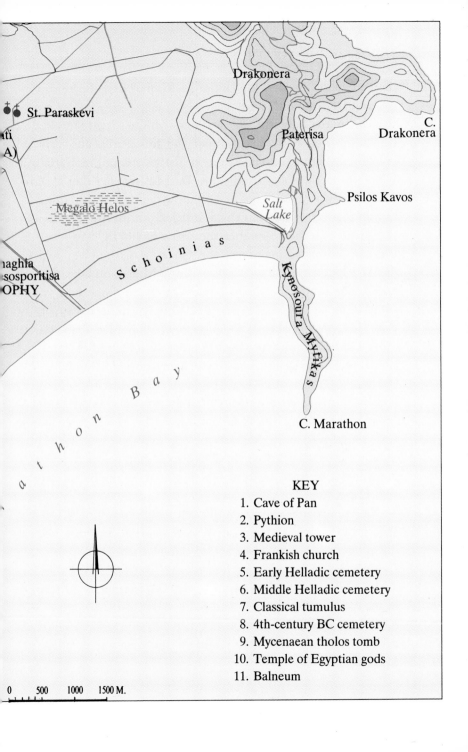

Drakonera

St. Paraskevi

C.
Drakonera

Paterisa

Megalo Helos

Salt
Lake

Psilos Kavos

naghia
sosporitisa
OPHY

S c h o i n i a s

Kynosoura Mytikas

M
a
r
a
t
h
o
n

B
a
y

C. Marathon

KEY

1. Cave of Pan
2. Pythion
3. Medieval tower
4. Frankish church
5. Early Helladic cemetery
6. Middle Helladic cemetery
7. Classical tumulus
8. 4th-century BC cemetery
9. Mycenaean tholos tomb
10. Temple of Egyptian gods
11. Balneum

0   500   1000   1500 M.

their existence are the inscriptions and marble dedications discovered from time to time.

The plain between the sea and Mount Stavrokoraki towards the northwest had neither the same area nor form in antiquity. The sea intruded much further inland, more than a kilometre as the subsoil indicates. In trial trenches dug at various points water spurts up at a shallow depth and the composition of the soil shows that this is a dried out marsh. The marsh was created in the years after the battle of 490 BC as a result of the continuous silting up of the Charadros, the river which, until the construction of the dam of the Marathon lake, flowed and flooded onto the plain. It seems that the large and sometimes destructive Charadros, as it is known in an ancient pro-

2 verb, is represented in a relief head of a bearded man, dated *circa* 470 BC. Found at Marathon, it was acquired by the Berlin Museum[4] in 1848, through the mediation of Schaubert, the German architect and town-planner of King Otto's Athens. Reliefs of this figure are regarded conventionally as personifications of the great river Acheloos. However, the find spot suggests some river in the Marathon area, and the most likely candidate is the Charadros. It is possible that a sanctuary was dedicated hereabouts, from which the relief in Berlin might well come.

The plain of Marathon is distinct from the rest of Attica on account of its wetlands and its lush vegetation. In the words of the ancient scholiast[5] it was ʽτῇ φύσει τραχύς, δισίππαστος, ἔχων ἐν ἑαυτῷ πηλούς, τενάγη, λίμνας (rugged, unsuitable for horses, full of mud, swamps and lakes). Aristophanes in *Birds*,[6] in the words of the hoopoe, summons those birds, ὅσα τ᾽ εὐδρόσους γῆς τόπους / ἔχετε λειμῶνα τ᾽ ἐρόεντα Μαραθῶνος (that nest in well-bedewed places and in the pleasing meadow at Marathon).

Fig. 2. Marble mask of a river god (Acheloos), in Berlin.

Just as today, large parts of the plain were cultivated. Indeed they were fertile and the earth was characterized as 'rich' (λιπαρὰ Μαραθών)[7] and 'full of olive trees',[8] τέμενος βαθύδενδρον ἐλαιοκόμου Μαραθῶνος.

Marathon owes its world-wide fame today and its outstanding place in the consciousness of the ancient Greeks —primarily of the Athenians who always spoke of it with reverence and respect— to the momentous battle between Athenians and Persians fought on the plain in 490 BC. The description of this battle in the following pages relies on information from the ancient authors and poets.

7

The Battle of Marathon

The conflict

After its capture and destruction of Eretria in 490 BC, the Persian army led by Datis sailed down the south Euboean strait, in the fleet commanded by Artaphernes, and landed on the coast of Marathon, striking camp along what is now the Schoinia beach. According to Herodotus, the Persians decided to disembark and encamp here on the advice of Hippias, the exiled son of the tyrant Pisistratos, who was accompanying the invaders. Hippias believed that the rural population of the Marathon region would receive him favourably because the farmers there still had good memories of the Pisistratids' regime. Furthermore, the large plain lent itself to the movement and manoeuvres of the Persian cavalry, which was to take part in the engagement with the Athenians.[9]

The Persians intended to cross Attica and besiege Athens. As soon as the *strategoi* (generals) in Athens learnt of this plan, they sent a herald to Sparta to ask for help, the *hemerodromos* (long-distance runner) Philippides. Despite the warm entreaties of this emissary, the Spartans could not respond immediately to the Athenians' request, for religious reasons. '...for it was the ninth day of the first part of the month, and they would make no expedition (they said) on the ninth day, when the moon was not full. So they waited for the full moon. As for the Persians, they were guided to Marathon by Hippias son of Pisistratus'.[10] The Pisistratid believed that the Persian enterprise would have a favourable outcome, because 'Hippias in the past night had seen a vision in his sleep, wherein he thought that he lay with his own mother; he interpreted this dream to signify that he should return to Athens and recover his power, and so die an old man in his own mother-country'.[11]

So the Persian fleet arrived at Marathon and Hippias began to array the barbarians. During this operation something happened that had quite the opposite portent to the dream. As Herodotus relates,[12] 'Now while he dealt with these matters he fell a-sneezing and a-coughing more violently than he was wont; he was well stricken in years, and the most of his teeth were loose; whereby the violence of his cough made one of his teeth to fall out. It fell into the sand, and Hippias used all diligence to find it; but the tooth being nowhere to be seen, he said lamentably to them that stood by, "This land is none of ours, nor shall we avail to subdue it; my tooth has all the share of it that was for me" '.

There was nothing fortuitous about the choice of Marathon as the venue for the Persian landing. It was suitable for the Persian cavalry and there was food and water, but for Hippias, whose sights were set on gaining power, there was a special reason. It was from here that his father, Pisistratos, had set off in 546 BC to establish the third tyranny in Athens, and so he believed that the people there were friendly towards him.[13] The Athenians, at Miltiades' instigation, acted boldly and mobilized against the invaders. They sped to face them, determined to stem their projected advance across Attica and attack on Athens by land, while the Persian fleet would be anchored at Phaleron. They encamped near the *Heracleion*, the sanctuary of Heracles at Marathon. Aristotle speaks of the decree issued by the Athenians, on the proposal of Miltiades, in the following words:[14] '*ἐπισιτισαμένους ἔφη δεῖν ἐξιέναι τὸ Μιλτιάδου ψήφισμα*' (to set off once they have obtained food). Only the Plataeans sped to their aid, with 1,000 warriors. The Athenian force totalled some 10,000 men and was commanded by ten *strategoi* (generals), among them Miltiades. Eleventh was the *polemarchos* (commander-in-chief) Callimachus from Aphidnae, whom Miltiades persuaded to accept his battle plan. Herodotus has preserved Miltiades' words:[15] ' "Callimachus", said he, "it is for you to-day to choose, whether you will enslave Athens or free her and thereby leave such a memorial for all posterity as was left not even by Harmodius and Aristogeiton. For now is Athens in greater peril than ever since she was first a city; and if her people bow their necks to the Medes, their fate is certain, for they will be delivered over to Hippias; but if our city be saved, she may well grow to be the first of Greek cities. How then this can be brought about, and how it comes that the deciding voice in these matters is yours, I will now show you. We ten generals are divided in counsel, some bidding us to fight and some to forebear. Now if we forebear to fight, it is likely that some great schism will rend and shake the courage of our people till they make friends of the Medes; but if we join battle before some at Athens be infected by corruption, then let heaven but deal fairly with us, and we may well win in this fight. It is you that all this concerns; all hangs on you; for if you join yourself to my opinion, you make your country free and your city the first in Hellas; but if you choose the side of them that would persuade us not to fight, you will have wrought the very opposite of the blessings whereof I have spoken" '.

Callimachus espoused Miltiades' views and the generals

voted to do battle with the Persians.[16] 'Thereafter the generals whose counsel was for fighting made over to Miltiades the day's right of leading that fell to each severally; he received it, but would not join battle till the day his own leadership came round'.

When his turn came, Miltiades ranged the troops in the following manner, ready to fight the Persians:[17] 'The right wing was commanded by Callimachus the polemarch; for it was then the Athenian custom that the holder of that office should have the right wing. He being there captain, next to him came the tribes one after another in the order of their numbers; last of all the Plataeans were posted on the left wing. Ever since that fight, when the Athenians bring sacrifices to the assemblies that are held at the five-yearly festivals, the Athenian herald prays that all blessings may be granted to Athenians and Plataeans alike. But now, when the Athenians were arraying at Marathon, it so fell out that their line being equal in length to the Median, the middle part of it was but a few ranks deep, and here the line was weakest, each wing being strong in numbers.

Their battle being arrayed and the omens of sacrifice favouring, straightway the Athenians were let go and charged the Persians at a run. There was between the armies a space of not less than eight furlongs. When the Persians saw them come running they prepared to receive them, deeming the Athenians frenzied to their utter destruction, who being (as they saw) so few were yet charging them at speed, albeit they had no horsemen nor archers. Such was the imagination of the foreigners; but the Athenians, closing all together with the Persians, fought in memorable fashion'.

Nothing on the plain of Marathon today hints at the momentous battle of 490 BC. The ten thousand Athenians and

Plataeans, outnumbered several times by the Persian foe, the slaves, fought desperately in the September sun, shrouded in an immense cloud of dust. The war cries, the commands, the anguished groans of the wounded and dying, the clash of shields, swords and spears created a preternatural atmosphere. Herodotus describes the battle in very few words, with striking terseness considering its duration:[18] μαχομένων δὲ ἐν τῷ Μαραθῶνι χρόνος ἐγίνετο πολλὸς (for a long time they fought at Marathon). This phrase should not be interpreted by modern standards, where the clash between men takes place after a protracted barrage of artillery fire. The battle of Marathon lasted[19] about one hour. The battle of Agincourt (25 October 1415) lasted an hour and a half and of Waterloo (18 June 1815) from 11 a.m. to 8.30 p.m.

Historical research has shown that, contrary to Herodotus' account, hostilities were initiated by the Persians. In order to repel the assault the Athenians moved against them towards the plain, indeed at the end they charged at a run because the enemy arrows were falling thick and fast. Herodotus says:[20] 'for they [the Athenians] were the first Greeks, within my knowledge, who charged their enemies at a run, and the first who endured the sight of the Median garments and men clad therein; till then, the Greeks were affrighted by the very name of the Medes'.

The Athenian centre, its weakest point, was driven back under the onslaught of the Persians and Sacae, but on the stronger wings the Athenians and Plataeans were victorious. They encircled the centre and reversed the Athenians' setback. The Persians withdrew, despite their strong defence, to near the Charadros torrent on the plain, and managed to board their ships, seven of which were taken by the Athenians. 'The foreigners overcame the middle part of the line, against which the

Persians themselves and the Sacae were arrayed; here the foreigners prevailed and broke the Greeks, pursuing them inland. But on either wing the Athenians and the Plataeans were victorious; and being so, they suffered the routed of their enemies to fly, and drew their wings together to fight against those that had broken the middle of their line; and here the Athenians had their victory, and followed after the Persians in their flight, hewing them down, till they came to the sea. There they called for fire and laid hands on the ships'.[21]

Herodotus records a supernatural event,[22] concerning Epizelus, a blinded warrior of 490 BC. 'And it fell out that a marvellous thing happened: a certain Athenian, Epizelus son of Cuphagoras, while he fought doughtily in the mellay lost the sight of his eyes, albeit neither stabbed in any part nor shot, and for the rest of his life continued blind from that day. I heard that he told the tale of this mishap thus: a tall man-at-arms (he said) encountered him, whose beard spread all over his shield; this apparition passed Epizelus by, but slew his neighbour in the line. Such was the tale Epizelus told, as I heard'. And the traveller Pausanias[23] heard a similar story from the inhabitants of Marathon. During the course of the battle a peasant appeared, a man of rustic appearance and dress, who slew many of the barbarians with a plough he was holding and then disappeared. Curious as to the identity of their unknown ally, the Athenians later inquired of Apollo at Delphi, who merely replied that they should honour the hero *Echetlaios* (ἐχέτλη = plough-tail). That this story was generated in the hour of battle and believed to be true, as is apparent from the fact that the Athenians depicted the hero Echetlus in the great wall-painting of the battle of Marathon in the Poikile (Painted) Stoa in the Agora at Athens, work of the painter Panainos (first half of 5th century BC). The great Attic hero Theseus is also said to have taken part in the battle. Plutarch,[24] in the *Life* dedicated to him, recounts ῾τῶν ἐν Μαραθῶνι πρὸς Μήδους μαχομένων ἔδοξαν οὐκ ὀλίγοι φάσμα Θησέως ἐν ὅπλοις καθορᾶν πρὸ αὐτῶν ἐπὶ τοὺς βαρβάρους φερόμενον᾽ (many of those who fought against the Medes at Marathon believed they had seen the spectre of panoplied Theseus before them rushing against the foreigners). This fancy too was evidently created in the hour of battle. In recognition of his contribution to their victory, the Athenians depicted Theseus in the wall-painting in the Poikile Stoa. A similarly strange tale is preserved by Aelian (2nd-3rd century AD): ῾συστρατιώτην δέ τις ᾽Αθηναῖος ἐν τῇ μάχῃ τῇ ἐν Μαραθῶνι ἐπήγετο κύνα, καὶ γραφῇ εἴκασται ἐν τῇ Ποικίλῃ ἑκάτερος, μὴ ἀτιμασθέντος τοῦ κυνός, ἀλλὰ ὑπὲρ τοῦ κινδύνου μισθὸν εἰληφότος ὁρᾶσθαι σὺν τοῖς ἀμφὶ τὸν Κυνέγειρον καὶ ᾽Επίζηλόν τε καὶ Καλλίμαχον. ἔστι δὲ καὶ οὗτοι καὶ ὁ κύων Μίκωνος γράμμα. οἱ δὲ οὐ τούτου, ἀλλὰ τοῦ Θασίου Πολυγνώτου φασίν᾽[25] (some Athenian had a dog with him at the battle of Marathon; and they are both painted in the Poikile Stoa. The dog showed valour and for the danger he was put in he received as reward his depiction among those surrounding Cynegirus, Epizelus and Callimachus. All these and the dog have been painted by Micon. Others say that they were not painted by Micon but by Polygnotus from Thasos). If the tale is true, the dog of the anonymous Athenian must have been a large, ferocious creature that fought with its teeth against his master's adversaries. According to Herodotus,[26] the Persians lost some six thousand four hundred men, and the Athenians one hundred and ninety-two, some of whom he mentions by name: 'In this work was slain Callimachus the polemarch, after doing doughty deeds; there too died one of the generals, Stesilaus son of Thrasylus; moreover, Cynegirus son of Euphorion fell there, his hand smitten off by an axe as he laid hold of a ship's poop, and many other famous Athenians'.

The renowned Persian cavalry —or at least not all— did not take part in the battle. An ancient testimony is preserved in the Byzantine *Souda* dictionary. In his interpretation of the proverbial phrase 'χωρὶς ἱππεῖς' (the horsemen, the cavalry, was separate, far away) the lexicographer gives the following information on the hours before the battle: 'The horsemen at a distance. When Datis invaded Attica, they say that the Ionians, when he left, climbed up the trees and made signs to the Athenians that the horsemen were far away; Miltiades, realizing the significance of their absence, attacked and was victorious; so this proverb is said of those who dissolve their formation'.

A modern explanation for the absence of the cavalry is its supposed tardiness in returning from the place where it was grazing and watering. This was due to the delayed setting of the moon on the night of the 16th to the 17th day of the lunar month, that is the day of the battle, which deceived the grooms about the hour of return.[27] On that day the moon set after dawn. Nevertheless, part of the cavalry did fight in the battle; this is attested indirectly by Pausanias[28] and directly by Cornelius Nepos,[29] as well as by representations in works of art.[30]

The betrayal

The withdrawal of the Persians, who sailed towards Phaleron intent on conquering Athens, is linked with another incident also narrated by Herodotus.[31] The Athenians regarded the Alcmeonids as responsible for this move by the Persians, the result of a deal between them; '... the Alcmeonidae [a powerful political family in Athens], it was said, made a compact with the Persians and held up a shield for them to see when they were now on shipboard'. Further on in his account, however,[32] the same historian rejects the accusation rife among the Athenians of treachery by the Alcmeonids, though he confirms the event of the raising of the shield: 'ἀνεδέχθη μὲν γὰρ ἀσπίς, καὶ τοῦτο οὐκ ἔστι ἄλλως εἰπεῖν· ἐγένετο γάρ· ὃς μέντοι ἦν ὁ ἀναδέξας, οὐκ ἔχω προσωτέρω εἰπεῖν τούτων' (indeed a shield was held aloft, and that cannot be denied; for the thing was done; but who did it I know not, and can say no further). The shield of which Herodotus speaks was not the familiar defensive weapon, unsuitable for signalling, but a flat, burnished bronze disc from which it was possible to flash the sun's rays from a considerable distance to a specific target.

Herodotus' account

Our principal source about the conduct of the battle is the
3 account of the historian Herodotus from Halicarnassus, who has been dubbed 'the Father of History'. His narrative, written *circa* 455-445 BC, is based on oral testimonies, inscriptions and monuments. An ancient anecdote relates[33] that when he was reading his history aloud in Athens the young Thucydides, who was among the audience, burst into tears. Herodotus saw the boy and said to his father: 'ὦ Ὄλορε, ὀργᾷ ἡ φύσις τοῦ υἱοῦ σου πρὸς μαθήματα' (Olorus, your son's nature yearns for lessons).

Fig. 3. Bust of Herodotus (Naples Museum no. 6239).

Certainly Herodotus obtained his information about the battle from genuine veterans. Many were still alive in Aristophanes' day (425 BC) and the great comic poet describes some of them:[34] 'οἱ δ' ὤσφροντο πρεσβῦταί τινες / 'Αχαρνικοί, σιπτοὶ γέροντες πρίνινοι / ἀτεράμονες Μαραθωνομάχαι σφενδάμνινοι' (But some old men smelt me, Acharnians, tough, sturdy, inexorable, hewn from holm oak, with hearts of maple, old warriors of Marathon).

One of those who fought in the battle was Epizelus son of Cuphagoras, who has been mentioned already. It was from him that Herodotus learnt of the remarkable apparition in the vision which cost him his sight. Aspersions have been cast on the

17

veracity of Herodotus' information. It is argued that thirty-five
to forty years after the battle those who took part in it were at
least 60 years old and had perhaps formed their own picture of
the great conflict. Undoubtedly in moments such as the battle
of Marathon many events are magnified and acquire a supernatural dimension, Epizelus' tale being a case in point; however, the belief in the existence of supernatural phenomena and
interventions is itself proof of the glorious import the struggle
acquired for those who were there, something we know of well
from the Albanian Campaign of 1940. The battle of 490 BC
was a gigantic engagement. Alone and for the first time, the
Athenians faced the famed Persian warriors. Their impressions
of the clash corresponded to its size and significance.

The Tumulus of the Athenians

The brief description of the terrain in the area of Marathon
and the other three demes of the Tetrapolis begins from the
4 *Soros*, the great mound of earth[35] that covered the 192 Athenian dead, who fell fighting against the Persian foe in September
490 BC.

The Tumulus ($Τύμβος$) of the Athenians is the main monument in the region and revered worldwide. The cremation and
burial of the slain warriors on the field of battle was a special
honour accorded by the Athenian state to the defenders of
Greek liberty. The present dimensions of the tumulus are
height 9 m, perimeter 185 m and diameter 50 m. Its form is not
exactly the same as in antiquity: there has been continuous ero-

Fig. 4. The tumulus of the Athenians.

sion and deposition of soil, and excavations made there in the past were subsequently filled in.

In his account of the burial of the dead from the first year of the Peloponnesian War, the historian Thucydides[36] says that the cypress-wood coffins with the remains: '...are laid in the public sepulchre, which is situated in the most beautiful suburb of the city; there they always bury those fallen in war, except indeed those who fell at Marathon; for their valour the Athenians judged to be pre-eminent and they buried them on the spot where they fell'.

So the Athenian dead were buried on the battlefield. But Thucydides does not reveal how. Pausanias states more precisely[37] that the Athenians were buried in a grave upon which stelae were erected with the names of the dead listed according to tribe. The Athenians of the Hellenistic era[38] named the place where the fallen were buried the *polyandrion*. This same word was used at the end of the first century BC to characterize the tomb of those slain in the naval battle of Salamis.[39]

Some historians and archaeologists doubt whether the Tumulus covers the Athenian dead or even whether it was formed after the burial or is a later accumulation of earth made to protect the destroyed graves. It is even believed that its construction may have been decided upon in a moment of national elation, to make the place of burial more imposing. However, the prevailing view today is that the great tumulus does indeed cover the remains of the Athenians killed in the battle. It occupies the site where the cremated remains of the corpses of the 192 wariors were collected and their relatives deposited vases as grave goods (*kterismata*). Earth was heaped upon them and the knoll we see today created.

Each of the 192 victims was cremated separately. The relatives, who had hastened from Athens taking with them household ornaments to deposit close to their dead, made their own arrangements for the funerary rites. This is apparent first from the fact that the vases in the tumulus have not suffered the effect of fire. In any case it was for obvious reasons impractical to burn 192 corpses in the same place at the same time. A picture of the cremation of several corpses simultaneously is given in the *Iliad* (I 52). After the slaying by Apollo, on the invocation of the priest Chryses, of many Danaans, their camp was filled with funeral pyres: '*αἰεὶ δὲ πυραὶ νεκύων καίοντο θαμειαί*' (and ever did the pyres of the dead burn thick). The battlefield full of pyres, with the relatives mourning around each must have presented the same picture. When the pyres had died down the relatives gathered the remains of their loved one and deposited them on the site of the Tumulus, where a few outstanding soldiers, such as the polemarch Callimachus, may have been cremated.

Aristides and the hoplites of the Antiochis tribe had remained on the battlefield with their accompanying slaves, who took part in the burial of the 192 Athenians and the Persians.

Pausanias relates[40] that stelae bearing the names of the dead according to tribes were set up on the grave: ῾τάφος δὲ ἐν τῷ πεδίῳ ᾿Αθηναίων ἐστίν, ἐπὶ δὲ αὐτῷ στῆλαι τὰ ὀνόματα τῶν ἀποθανόντων κατὰ φυλὰς ἑκάστων ἔχουσαι᾿ (on the plain is the grave of the Athenians, and upon it are slabs giving the names of the killed according to their tribes). Ten stelae were not necessarily erected, there may have been fewer. The mention of the dead of each tribe obligatorily followed the official order, with which we are familiar. The Plataean dead and the slaves were buried somewhere else on the battlefield.

As the same traveller writes,[41] Diaeus, the general of the Achaean Confederacy in 146 BC: ῾καὶ δούλους τε ἐς ἐλευθερίαν ἠφίει, τὸ Μιλτιάδου καὶ ᾿Αθηναίων βούλευμα πρὸ τοῦ ἔργου τοῦ ἐν Μαραθῶνι μιμούμενος᾿ (proceeded to set free slaves, following the example of Miltiades and the Athenians before the battle of Marathon). So in this battle in 490 BC slaves fought for the first time. A monument (cenotaph) was later erected on the battlefield for Miltiades, the victorious *strategos*. Pausanias preserves[42] a local tradition: 'At Marathon every night you can hear horses neighing and men fighting'. This belief which prevailed among the inhabitants of Marathon is telling. Sixteen generations later the memory of the great battle was still alive and real.

The excavation of the Tumulus

Several mounds on the Marathon plain attracted the interest of foreign travellers in the Ottoman period. The Tumulus of the Athenians dominated, and W.M. Leake[43] was struck by the large number of obsidian blades scattered hereabouts. The first excavation was conducted by H. Schliemann in 1884, with the Ephor of Antiquities Demetrios Philios as supervisor. This venture failed because water welled up in the excavated sector, and was soon abandoned. Indeed in his publication[44] Schliemann maintained that the tumulus was much earlier than the battle and was not connected with it, which view was espoused by D. Philios.[45]

The final investigation was carried out on behalf of the General Ephorate of Antiquities by Ephor Valerios Stais,[46] in 1890 and 1891. A thick layer of charcoal and ash was found, and charred skeletal remains which disintegrated when touched. Stais also revealed a structure of unbaked bricks orientated North-South, that is a man-made ditch. This was a *bothros*, the place where the remains of the funerary banquets consumed on the site of the tumulus during the burial of the dead, and the vessels used at these, were deposited. This *bothros*, 5 m long and 1 m wide according to Stais' publication, yielded ash from fire and abundant food residues, that is bones of animals and birds, as well as egg shells. Scattered along its entire length were fragments of vases, indeed of the vases in the National Archaeological Museum, Athens, 1036 (amphora, work of the vase-painter Sophilos), 766 (lopas), 764a (pyxis), 762a (amphora), as well as kylix 848 in the Marathon Museum. The degree of destruction of these vases indicates that they were smashed intentionally, so as not to be used again, for they be-

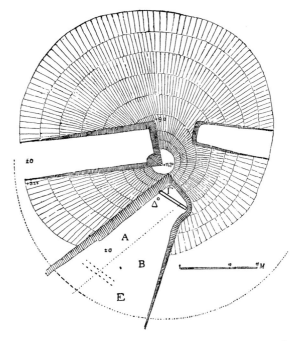

Fig. 5. Plan of the excavation of the tumulus of the Athenians (V. Stais, AM 18, 1893, 49).

longed to the dead after they had been used on the spot by the relatives of the fallen during the funerary meal, the so-called *perideipnon* (the equivalent of today's funerary repast held in the home of the deceased or of the relatives).

Over the remains of the dead that had been gathered together on the site of the tumulus, the relatives scattered numerous cheap vases, black-figure lekythoi purchased from some shop in Marathon. These last bear no traces of fire and constitute the ultimate offering to the 192 Athenians.

A few of the vases in the *bothros* are much earlier than the battle of Marathon. There is nothing strange about this since some relatives of the dead who hurried to Marathon from Athens or other parts of Attica took with them whatever vessel they considered worthy of burying beside their loved one. The Sophilos amphora, the pyxis 764a and the amphora 762a were kept in the homes of the dead warriors as family heirlooms, inherited from their fathers or grandfathers.

The grave of the Persians

The Persian dead were buried in a mass grave on the battle field, near where the church of the Panaghia (Virgin) Mesosporitissa now stands. This is deduced from information given by the German Captain Eschenburg who, in the winter of 1884/85, mapped the region of Marathon. He records[47] that 'in the vineyard belonging to Skouzes a large quantity of remains of bones was found, haphazardly placed, which seems to belong to hundreds of dead. I thank for the information Mr Skouzes' steward, a clever young Greek under whose direction the vineyard was planted. I myself dug at the edges of the vineyard and ascertained that this area full of remains of bones extends as far as the marshes'.

Herodotus informs us[48] of the number of Persian dead: '*ἐν ταύτῃ τῇ ἐν Μαραθῶνι μάχῃ ἀπέθανον τῶν βαρβάρων κατὰ ἑξακισχιλίους καὶ τετρακοσίους ἄνδρας*' (In this fight at Marathon there were slain of the foreigners about six thousand four hundred men).

Centuries later, some 640 years after the great battle, the traveller Pausanias[49] could find no sign of the grave of the Persians: 'τοὺς δὲ Μήδους ᾿Αθηναῖοι μὲν θάψαι λέγουσιν, ὡς πάντως ὅσιον ἀνθρώπου νεκρὸν γῇ κρύψαι, τάφον δὲ οὐδένα εὑρεῖν ἠδυνάμην· οὔτε γὰρ χῶμα οὔτε ἄλλο σημεῖον ἦν ἰδεῖν, ἐς ὄρυγμα δὲ φέροντες σφᾶς ὡς τύχοιεν ἐσέβαλον' (although the Athenians assert that they buried the Persians, because in every case the divine law applies that a corpse should be laid under the earth, yet I could find no grave. There was neither mound not other trace to be seen as the dead were carried to a trench and thrown in anyhow).

According to literary tradition Miltiades had promised Artemis Agrotera that the Athenians would sacrifice after their victory a goat for every Persian killed. The sophist Claudius Aelian (2nd-3rd century AD) mentions Miltiades' wish in one of his works:[50] '᾿Πέρσαι δὲ ἡττήθησαν τῇ ἡμέρᾳ ταύτῃ (τῇ ἕκτῃ τοῦ Θαργηλιῶνος) καὶ ᾿Αθηναῖοι δὲ τῇ ᾿Αγροτέρᾳ ἀποθύουσι τὰς χιμαίρας τὰς τριακοσίας κατὰ τὴν εὐχὴν τοῦ Μιλτιάδου δρῶντες τοῦτο' (The Persians were defeated on that day (the sixth of Thargelion) and the Athenians sacrificed to Agrotera three hundred billy goats, acting in accordance with Miltiades' wish). The same story was told several centuries earlier by the historian Xenophon, who explains[51] that because the Athenians could not find as many goats as the Persian dead, they decided to sacrifice five hundred a year (ἐπεὶ οὐκ εἶχον ἱκανὰς εὑρεῖν, ἔδοξεν αὐτοῖς κατ᾿ ἐνιαυτὸν πεντακοσίας θύειν, καὶ ἔτι νῦν ἀποθύουσιν).

The Athenians honoured Artemis in another way too. On the reverse of the silver tetradrachms[52] minted after the battle, **6** left of the head of the owl is the waning moon, at once symbol-

Fig. 6. Tetradrachm commemorating the battle of Marathon.

izing the time of the engagement and alluding to the assistance of the goddess whom the ancient Greeks regarded as the personification of the moon, just as her brother Apollo was of the sun.

The trophy

As soon as the battle was over, the Athenians set up on the field of Marathon a trophy, comprising a heap of the weapons and other spoils taken from the vanquished Medes. As the great Cyrus had told[53] his soldiers, these belonged to the victors: 'τὰ τῶν νικωμένων πάντα τοῖς νικῶσιν ἀεὶ ἄθλα πρόκειται'. Part of the booty was dedicated to the gods; the rest was the property of the Athenian state.

Themistocles' rival, Aristides, another of the ten generals who had conceded the leadership to Miltiades, was associated with the spoils. When the Athenians decided to return to Athens to confront the Persian fleet, which was planning to capture the city, they left behind on the field Aristides with the men of his tribe, the Antiochid, to guard the prisoners and the plunder. Plutarch narrates:[54] 'At Marathon Aristides remained as guard of the prisoners and the booty, with the men of his tribe, and he did not belie the opinion prevailing about him. Though there was a heap of gold and silver, and of every kind of luxurious garment, with countless goods in the tents and the captured ships, neither he desired to take anything, nor did he allow anyone, apart from a few who escaped his attention, to take advantage. Among these was Callias the torch-bearer'.

The trophy of the battle, a famous monument in antiquity, is briefly described by Pausanias:[55] 'A trophy too of white marble has been erected'. The remains of it are preserved incorpor- **7** ated in the walls of a Medieval tower very near the Panaghia Mesosporitissa, the church dedicated to the Presentation of the Virgin (21 November), at the southwest edge of the Large Marsh. The most important remnant of the trophy is an Ionic column capital bearing a trapezoidal hollow on its upper surface, on which a marble statue was placed. A few unfluted drums of the column survive, and a much eroded fragment of marble on which traces of the drapery of a garment are preserved, is attributed to the statue. The capital and drums are **8** dated after the Persian Wars, to the second quarter of the fifth century BC. Athenian authors of the fifth century BC already speak of the monument with pride. Aristophanes mentions it three times.[56] Critias, the harshest of the thirty tyrants, praises Athens in one of his elegies:[57] 'ἡ τὸ καλὸν Μαραθῶνι καταστή-σασα τρόπαιον' (that set up at Marathon the beautiful trophy). Plato, in *Menexenus*, refers[58] to the virtue of those who fought at Marathon, who: 'having suffered the force of the barbarians and punished the arrogance of the whole of Asia, and having first set up a trophy to their victories over the barbarians, first showed and taught the other Greeks that the might of the Persians is not invincible, but that any crowd of men and any wealth, is subject to the rules of valour'.

Herodotus is laconic in his description of the battle. From the sophist Polemon (1st-2nd century AD), who composed funerary orations to Cynegiros and Callimachus, it is ascertained[59] that over the years a lore had been woven concerning the battle and the protagonists' deeds. The dead Callimachus, his upright body covered with Persian arrows, terrified the barbarians: *'βασιλεὺς δὲ ἰδὼν αὐτὸν ὀρθὸν ὅπλοις πολλοῖς πε-*

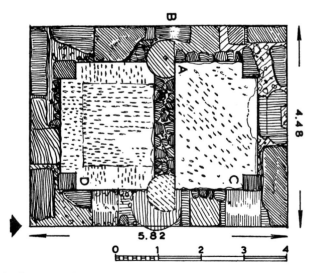

Fig. 7. Plan of the medieval tower at the Virgin Mesosporitissa (I. Travlos).

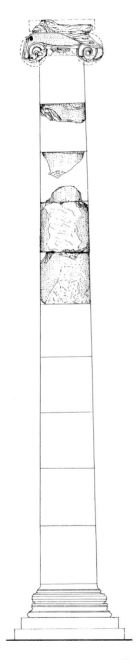

Fig. 8. Reconstruction of the trophy of the battle of Marathon (I. Yarmenitis).

0   1   2 μ

ριβεβλημένον ἐβόα· φεύγωμεν, πλέωμεν· ἤδη γὰρ ἤγειραν
'Αθηναῖοι τρόπαιον' (On seeing him struck by arrows, the Persian king cried out: Let's leave, let's cast away; the Athenians
set up a trophy).

The announcement of the victory

The story of the Athenian hoplite who, when the battle was
over, sped fully armed to Athens, to announce the victory, is
familiar from the author Heracleides Ponticus (4th century
BC). Plutarch from Chaeronea (1st-2nd century AD) draws on
the now lost work of Heracleides and repeats the tale in one of
his essays:[60] 'Τὴν τοίνυν ἐν Μαραθῶνι μάχην ἀπήγγειλεν, ὡς
μὲν Ἡρακλείδης ὁ Ποντικὸς ἱστορεῖ, Θέρσιππος ὁ Ἐρχιεύς· οἱ
δὲ πλεῖστοι λέγουσιν Εὐκλέα δραμόντα σὺν τοῖς ὅπλοις θερμὸν
ἀπὸ τῆς μάχης καὶ ταῖς θύραις ἐμπεσόντα τῶν πρώτων τοσοῦτον
μόνον εἰπεῖν "χαίρετε, νικῶμεν", εἶτ' εὐθὺς ἐκπνεῦσαι' (The
news of the victory at Marathon was announced, as narrated
by Heracleides from Pontus, by Thersippos the Erchieus; however most historians say that Eucles ran in panoply and sweat-
ing from the battle, and as he reached the doors of the city's
archons, all he could say was "Hail! we are victorius!" and he
immediately passed away).

Lucian from Samosata in Commagene (2nd century AD)
draws on a different historical source, narrating the same
event[61] with minor differences: 'Πρῶτος δ' αὐτὸ Φιλιππίδης ὁ
ἡμεροδρομήσας λέγεται ἀπὸ Μαραθῶνος ἀγγέλλων τὴν νίκην
εἰπεῖν πρὸς τοὺς ἄρχοντας καθημένους καὶ πεφροντικότας ὑπὲρ
τοῦ τέλους τῆς μάχης, χαίρετε, νικῶμεν, καὶ τοῦτο εἰπὼν συν-

αποθανεῖν τῇ ἀγγελίᾳ καὶ τῷ χαίρειν συνεκπνεῦσαι' (It is said that Philippides was the first to run from Marathon to announce the victory, he said to the archons who were assembled worried about the outcome of the battle 'Joy to you, we've won', and while telling the tidings he died, his last breath expiring with the 'Joy to you'). There was of course a quicker way of announcing the momentous news, by signals, a system used by soldiers in order to pass on information about enemy movements. Without doubt this was how the Athenians learnt of the sack of Eretria and the Persians' landing at Marathon. Assuming Plutarch's and Lucian's story is true, it would have taken the Athenian hoplite, already exhausted by the battle, several hours to reach Athens. The British historian Nicholas Hammond, a young student in Athens in 1930, wishing to clarify some practical problems regarding the battle, went on foot from Marathon to Athens, by way of Penteli, in six hours. Fatigued from walking, he returned immediately via the same mountain route in seven hours.[62] Modern Marathon runners cover the distance on the road via Nea Makri-Rafina-Pallini in less than three hours.

As we have seen, the name of the herald varies. Plutarch, following Heracleides Ponticus, calls him *Thersippos* or *Eucles*, the majority view. Lucian hands down a third name, *Philippides*. This was the name[63] of the *hemerodromos* sent to Sparta as emissary before the battle, to ask for assistance. Thus it is implied that after returning from Sparta Philippides was present at Marathon, and that it was he who, by virtue of his status as an *hemerodromos*, was accorded the privilege of running to Athens to announce the victory, a feat which cost him his life. However, Plutarch's version should be regarded as the more reliable.

In remembrance of the legendary achievement of the Athenian hoplite in 490 BC, the Marathon race was established in the modern Olympic games. At the first of these, held in Athens in 1896, the event was sponsored by the French professor Michel Bréal. It was won by Spyros Louis, in a time of 2 hours 59′ 50″. The distance of the Marathon course then was 40 km. The regular distance now is 42 km and 195 m, though it varies slightly depending on prevailing local conditions.

The Spartans, whose help the Athenians had sought, arrived in Athens after the full moon. The two thousand hoplites had marched at the double and reached the city within three days of their departure from Sparta. Though by the time they came the battle was over, they wanted to see the dead Medes. So they proceeded to Marathon, inspected the slain and the booty, and after praising the Athenians and their magnificent achievement, returned home.[64]

Ex-votos at Delphi

The Athenians used the tithe of the spoils of the battle to build in the sanctuary of Apollo at Delphi the so-called *Athen-*
9 *ian Treasury*, the little Doric temple (*naiskos*) known to all. It both expressed their gratitude to the Delphic god and housed their *ex-votos*. The sculpted decoration of the Amazonomachy on the metopes of the façade symbolized the triumph at Marathon and the struggle against the barbarian invader.

Along the length of the Athenian Treasury is a platform on which stands a long base bearing the inscription[65] ᾿Αθεναῖοι τ[ō]ι ᾿Απόλλον[ι ἀπὸ Μέδ]ον ἀκ[ροθ]ίνια τες Μαραθ[ō]νι μ[ά-χες] (The Athenians dedicate to Apollo the tenth of the booty they took from the Medes during the battle of Marathon). The

Fig. 9. The Athenian Treasury at Delphi.

Athenians' dedication was a series of bronze statues which probably portrayed Attic heroes.

This was not the only *ex-voto* of the victors to Apollo. Around 465 BC the Athenians dedicated a large group of statues, again in the sanctuary at Delphi. According to the description of the traveller Pausanias,[66] on the left side of the beginning of the Sacred Way they had set up 16 statues representing Athena, Apollo, the victor in the battle of Marathon Miltiades and ten Attic heroes, of which seven were the eponyms of the tribes of Athens. The many-figured sculpture was created by the great Phidias and was also paid for from the tithe of the spoils from Marathon. The non-eponymous heroes were Codrus, Theseus and Phyleus.

Later the statues of new eponymous heroes were added, of the kings of Macedon Antigonus and Demetrius (307/6 BC), and of Ptolemy III Euergetes of Egypt (224/3 BC), '*Tὸν μὲν Αἰγύπτιον καὶ εὐνοίᾳ τινὶ ἐς αὐτόν, τοὺς δὲ Μακεδόνας τῷ ἐς αὐτοὺς δέει*' (the statue of the Egyptian they sent out of goodwill; those of the Macedonians were sent because of the dread they inspired).

Ex-votos at Athens and Plataea

According to Pausanias[67] the great work of Phidias on the Acropolis, the bronze statue of Athena Promachos, was made from the tithe of the booty of the battle, '*ἀπὸ Μήδων τῶν ἐς Μαραθῶνα ἀποβάντων*' (from the Persians who landed at Marathon).

Around 460 BC Micon and Panainus painted in the Poikile Stoa at Athens the large mural depicting the battle of Marathon. Pausanias[68] describes the picture in detail. First from the left was Miltiades, urging his soldiers to rush against the barbarians, after this was the great engagement, the Persians' flight towards the morass, the Phoenician ships, the clash between Persians and Greeks near these, and the slaughter of the barbarians. Also depicted were Theseus, Athena and Heracles, the polemarch Callimachus and the hero Echetlus.

The Plataeans, who fought alongside their Athenian allies, also made their own dedications. Pausanias narrates[69] that a temple of Athena Areia (Warlike) was built at Plataea from their share of the booty. The goddess's statue was of gilded wood, but the face, hands and feet were of Pentelic marble. Slightly smaller than the bronze Athena Promachos, it too was sculpted by Phidias. At its feet stood the portrait statue of Arimnestos, who led the Plataeans at Marathon and in the subsequent battle of Plataea in 479 BC.

Legends and cults related to the battle

Various legends are linked with the victorious outcome of the battle. Pausanias[70] relates that 'The Marathonians worship both those who died in the fighting, calling them heroes, and secondly Marathon, from whom the parish derives its name, and then Heracles, saying that they were the first among the Greeks to acknowledge him as a god. They say too that there chanced to be present in the battle a man of rustic appearance and dress. Having slaughtered many of the foreigners with a plough he was seen no more after the engagement. When the Athenians made enquiries at the oracle the god merely ordered them to honour Echetlaeus (He of the Plough-tail) as a hero'.

Many centuries after the battle the memory of the favourable intervention of so many deities was vivid: of Marathon, Heracles, Echetlus, Theseus. The Athenians who had fallen were regarded as *heroes* and the valiant victory was attributed to divine intervention. The *ex-votos* and the sacrifices offered for centuries were the continuing expression of the Athenians' gratitude.

The battle was the reason for establishing the organized cult of a new god in Attica. As Herodotus narrates,[71] when Philippides, whom the Athenians sent to Sparta to ask for help, passed through the mountain Parthenion above Tegea, Pan called him by name and bade him tell the Athenians that they did not treat him as they ought, even though he was friendly towards them and had come to their aid several times in the past, and would do so in the future. The Athenians believed Philippides' tale and founded a sanctuary of Pan beneath the Acropolis. Indeed an epigram has survived,[72] attributed to the lyric poet Simonides of Ceos (556-468 BC) and mentioning a statue of Pan, *ex-voto* of the general Miltiades:

Τὸν τραγόπουν ἐμὲ Πᾶνα, τὸν Ἀρκάδα, τὸν κατὰ Μήδων,
τὸν μετ᾽ Ἀθηναίων, στήσατο Μιλτιάδης

(Miltiades erected me, the goat-footed Pan, the Arcadian, the enemy of the Medes, / the ally of the Athenians).

Pan is closely connected with Marathon, however, and his cult was observed there for many centuries after the battle of 490 BC. He was also worshipped in other parts of Attica, in the caves on Mounts Hymmetus, Pentele and Parnes, at Vari, Eleusis and Daphni. More will be said of him below.

All Greeks are familiar with the masterly epigram[73] of Simonides of Ceos on the Athenians' victory at Marathon.

Ἑλλήνων προμαχοῦντες Ἀθηναῖοι Μαραθῶνι
χρυσοφόρων Μήδων ἐστόρεσαν δύναμιν

(The Athenians fighting at Marathon, on behalf of all the Greeks, vanquished the force of the gold-clad Persians).

The epigram is quoted by the orator Lycurgus[74] and in the *Souda* dictionary.[75] It seems unlikely that it was inscribed on a stele on the battlefield.

The significance of the battle for posterity

The battle of Marathon was the most glorious event in the history of Athens and its importance was felt by Athenians of all eras. It was commemorated by the ancient authors, sculptors and painters who immortalized its scenes, and its protagonists were praised by poets.

A prize awarded to an athlete from Marathon at the first funerary games established by the Athenian state in honour of those slain in the battle, was a bronze cauldron with dotted **10** (pointillé) inscription[76] on the rim, according to which:

'Αθηναῖοι· ἆθλα ἐπὶ τοῖς ἐν τõι πολέμοι

(The Athenians offer it as a prize in the games in honour of those fallen in the war).

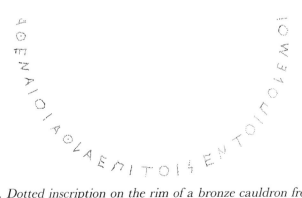

Fig. 10. Dotted inscription on the rim of a bronze cauldron from the area of the tumulus of the Athenians (Canellopoulos Museum no. 199, Athens).

The cauldron was found a short distance from the Tumulus of Marathon and contained charred bones. Since the inscription on it is dated to the 480s BC, it is quite possible that the unknown victor in the games was one of those who fought at the battle in 490 BC.

Games in honour of those killed in the wars against the Persians were established early on, and it was laid down that a funerary oration be delivered for those slain. According to the historian Diodorus Siculus[77] ὁ τῶν Ἀθηναίων δῆμος ἐκόσμησε τοὺς τάφους τῶν ἐν τῷ Περσικῷ πολέμῳ τελευτησάντων, καὶ τὸν ἀγῶνα τὸν ἐπιτάφιον τότε πρῶτον ἐποίησε, καὶ νόμον ἔθηκε λέγειν ἐγκώμια τοῖς δημοσίᾳ θαπτομένοις τοὺς προαιρεθέντας τῶν ῥητόρων' (The Athenians decorated the graves of those who fell in the war against the Persians, and then decided to hold the funeral games for the first time and voted a law that a speech be delivered in honour of those who were buried at the state's expense, by specially chosen orators).

The Athenians never ceased to honour both the battle and the 192 fellow citizens who fell there, with festivities and visits to the Tumulus. One such visit by the Athenian ephebes in the year when Demetrius was archon (123/2 BC) is recorded in an inscription[78] that says of these young men: 'they came to the cemetery of the fallen at Marathon and honoured with wreaths and funerary sacrifices those killed in the fight for freedom'. So we see that 367 years after the battle the memory of it was still intense and the Athenians honoured their ancestors who gave their life for the freedom of Hellas. Much later, Plutarch[79] narrates (*circa* AD 50-120) that the Athenians still celebrated the anniversary of the battle: 'Even now on the 6th of Boedromion [the month corresponds to September/October] the state celebrates the victory at Marathon'. It is calculated that the battle took place[80] in the morning of 11 September 490 BC. The orator and sophist Livanius[81] (4th century AD) remembered in a speech τὸν μετὰ λαμπάδων εἰς Μαραθῶνα δρόμον (the torch-race at Marathon) that took place in Alcibiades' day (5th century BC).

Greeks today likewise still remember those who died in the Fall of Constantinople (1453) and the War of Independence (1821), the heroes of Mesolongi, Souli, Alamana. Instead of Simonides and Aeschylus, they have Solomos and Calvos, for the struggles of the later Greeks were no different from those of their ancient ancestors, whom Solomos invokes as martyrs of national continuity: 'Rise up three hundred / and come back to us; / thy children want thee to see / how much they resemble thee'.

Miltiades

The leading figure in the battle of 490 BC, Miltiades, has been spoken of at various points in the account of the event. Born in 550 BC, he was eponymous archon of Athens in 524/23 BC,[82] having settled there after his campaign to the Chersonese. His enemies[83] 'ἐδίωξαν τυραννίδος τῆς ἐν Χερσονήσῳ· ἀποφυγὼν δὲ καὶ τούτοις στρατηγὸς οὕτως 'Αθηναίων ἀπεδέχθη, αἱρεθεὶς ὑπὸ τοῦ δήμου' (filed suit against him for his tyrannical rule in the Chersonese; and having been discharged of this accusation, he became general in Athens, elected by the people).

After the battle of Marathon he led an expeditionary force against Paros, but was unable to capture the island and so failed to fulfil his promises to the Athenians. He was tried and convicted for this offence, and fined 50 talents, which sum was paid after his death in prison, by his son Cimon.

A later epigram about Miltiades, of the second century AD, **11** has survived, incised on a herm bearing the general's head. The stele was found in the Villa Strozzi at Coelius in Rome and is nowadays housed in the National Museum, Ravenna. On its face is[84] this bilingual epigram:

> *Μιλτιάδης*
> *Qui Persas bello vicit Marathonis in arvis*
> *civibus ingratis et patria interit.*
> *Πάντες, Μιλτιάδη, τάδ᾽ ἀρήϊα ἔργα ἴσασιν,*
> *Πέρσαι καὶ Μαραθών, σῆς ἀρετῆς τέμενος.*

(He who vanquished the Persians in battle, on the field of Marathon, was ruined by ungrateful citizens and the fatherland. All, Miltiades, know of these martial feats, the Persians and Marathon, sanctuary of your valour).

Almost 700 years after the battle, this herm with the bust of the illustrious general, who by that time was a mythical figure, adorned the house of some citizen of Rome.

It has been suggested that on the Villa Strozzi herm we have a copy[85] of the head of the portrait statue of Miltiades set up by the Athenians in the theatre, together with one of Themistocles. Each statue was accompanied by a Persian captive, according to an ancient commentary in a speech[86] by Aelius

Fig. 11. Herm with bust of Miltiades (Ravenna Museum).

Aristeides: *'δύο εἰσὶν ἀνδριάντες ἐν τῷ 'Αθήνησι θεάτρῳ, ὁ μὲν ἐκ δεξιῶν Θεμιστοκλέους, ὁ δ' ἐξ εὐωνύμων Μιλτιάδου, πλησίον δὲ αὐτῶν ἑκατέρου Πέρσης αἰχμάλωτος'* (there are two statues in the theatre at Athens, that which stands on the right is of Themistocles, that on the left of Miltiades, and near each there is a statue of a Persian captive).

There was a statue of Miltiades, and one of Themistocles, in the Agora at Athens, close to the Prytaneion. In the time of the traveller Pausanias[87] the services of these two great men had evidently been forgotten, *'τὰς γὰρ Μιλτιάδου καὶ Θεμιστοκλέους εἰκόνας ἐς 'Ρωμαῖόν τε ἄνδρα καὶ Θρᾷκα μετέγραψαν'.* (For the likenesses of Miltiades and Themistocles have their titles changed to a Roman and a Thracian). The Athenians maintained that the Roman was Gaius Julius Nicanor, who was dubbed a 'new Themistocles', and the Thracian King Roimetalkes assumed[88] the figure of Miltiades.

For his contribution to the expulsion of the Persians from Greece the ancient Greeks regarded Miltiades as the first benefactor of Hellas. Pausanias,[89] speaking of Philopoemen, observes that *'καὶ ἤδη τὸ μετὰ τοῦτο ἐς ἀνδρῶν ἀγαθῶν φορὰν ἔληξεν ἡ 'Ελλάς. Μιλτιάδης μὲν γὰρ ὁ Κίμωνος τούς τε ἐς Μαραθῶνα ἀποβάντας τῶν βαρβάρων κρατήσας μάχῃ καὶ τὸν Μήδων ἐπισχὼν στόλον ἐγένετο εὐεργέτης πρῶτος κοινῇ τῆς 'Ελλάδος, Φιλοποίμην δὲ ὁ Κραύγιδος ἔσχατος'* (after this Greece ceased to bear good men. For Miltiades, the son of Cimon, overcame in battle the foreign invaders who had landed at Marathon, stayed the advance of the Persian army, and so became the first benefactor of all Greece, just as Philopoemen, the son of Craugis, was the last)'.

Two bronze helmets found in the great sanctuary at Olympia are associated with the battle of 490 BC. One, Greek, considerably eroded and incomplete, bears the dotted inscription

Μιλτιάδες [ἀ]νέ[θε]κεν [τõι Δί] (*Miltiades dedicated it to Zeus*). The other, 'Assyrian', conical and intact, bears the dotted inscription ἀθεναῖοι μέδον λαβόντες (the Athenians having taken from the Medes). The first is an *ex-voto*[90] of the general and the second of the city-state of Athens, from the booty of the defeated`Persians, that which Aristeides was put to guard after the battle.[91]

We do not know where Miltiades was buried. Many years after the battle a monument in his honour was erected at Ma-

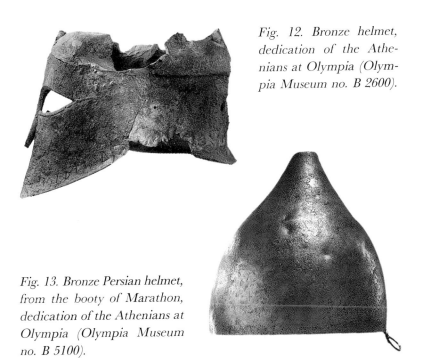

Fig. 12. Bronze helmet, dedication of the Athenians at Olympia (Olympia Museum no. B 2600).

Fig. 13. Bronze Persian helmet, from the booty of Marathon, dedication of the Athenians at Olympia (Olympia Museum no. B 5100).

rathon, in the most conspicuous position on the field. According to Pausanias[92] ‘καὶ ἀνδρός ἐστιν ἰδίᾳ μνῆμα Μιλτιάδου τοῦ Κίμωνος, συμβάσης ὕστερόν οἱ τῆς τελευτῆς Πάρου τε ἁμαρτόντι καὶ δι᾽ αὐτὸ ἐς κρίσιν ᾽Αθηναίους καταστάντι᾽ (there is also a separate monument to one man, Miltiades, the son of Cimon, although his end came later, after he had failed to take Paros and for this reason had been brought to trial by the Athenians). In the nineteenth century the remains of the medieval tower north of the Tumulus were considered to be the monument to Miltiades. This view, first expressed by Leake,[93] is untenable however, because the large, ashlar marble blocks of which the tower is built belonged to a sepulchral monument of the second half of the fourth century BC. Ross's view that this could have been the trophy erected by the Athenians after the battle is also untenable, for the same reasons.

Aeschylus the Marathon fighter

14 The towering figure in Attic tragedy, the poet Aeschylus (525/4-456 BC), was, like his brother Cynegeiros, one of the Athenians who fought at Marathon. Towards the end of his life he moved to Gela in Sicily, where he died, and on his tomb the Gelans incised the following epigram, said to have been composed by Aeschylus himself:[94]

Αἰσχύλον Εὐφορίωνος ᾽Αθηναῖον τόδε κεύθει
μνῆμα καταφθίμενον πυροφόροιο Γέλας·
ἀλκὴν δ᾽ εὐδόκιμον Μαραθώνιον ἄλσος ἂν εἴποι
καὶ βαθυχαιτήεις Μῆδος ἐπιστάμενος.

Fig. 14. Bust of the tragic poet Aeschylus.

(This tomb in wheat-bearing Gela covers the dead Aeschylus of Euphorion from Athens; the grove of Marathon can vouch for his famed valour, and the long-haired Mede who knew it well).

A great modern poet is also associated with this epigram, Constantine Cavafy. In his poem *Young Men of Sidon (400 AD)* he presents the imaginary objection of the poets of late antiquity to the precedence Aeschylus gave to his part in the battle of Marathon, in remembering only this in his epitaph and not his poetic *oeuvre*.

Cavafy does no more than remind us that the perplexity about Aeschylus' stance existed from very early times. Pausanias, in his wanderings in Athens, describes[95] the Eleusinion, a short way beyond which was 'ναὸς Εὐκλείας, ἀνάθημα καὶ τοῦτο ἀπὸ Μήδων, οἳ τῆς χώρας Μαραθῶνι ἔσχον. φρονῆσαι δὲ Ἀθηναίους ἐπὶ τῇ νίκῃ ταύτῃ μάλιστα εἰκάζω· καὶ δὴ καὶ Αἰσχύλος, ὥς οἱ τοῦ βίου προσεδοκᾶτο ἡ τελευτή, τῶν ἄλλων ἐμνημόνευσεν οὐδενός, δόξης ἐς τοσοῦτο ἥκων ἐπὶ ποιήσει καὶ πρὸ Ἀρτεμισίου καὶ ἐν Σαλαμῖνι ναυμαχήσας· ὁ δὲ τό τε ὄνομα πατρόθεν καὶ τὴν πόλιν ἔγραψε καὶ ὡς τῆς ἀνδρείας μάρτυρας ἔχοι τὸ Μαραθῶνι ἄλσος καὶ Μήδων τοὺς ἐς αὐτὸ ἀποβάντας' (... a temple to Eukleia (Glory), this too being a thank-offering for the victory over the Persians, who had landed at Marathon. This is the victory of which I am of the opinion that Athenians were proudest; while Aeschylus, who had won renown for his poetry and for his share in the naval battles before Artemisium and at Salamis, recorded at the prospect of his death nothing else, and merely wrote his name, his father's name and the name of his city, and added that he had witnesses to his valour in the grove at Marathon and in the Persians who landed there). The perplexity of the ancient Greeks first voiced by Pausanias was repeated by Athenaeus too.[96]

The polemarch Callimachus

The contribution of the polemarch Callimachus to the victory of 490 BC was important indeed. He was slain in the final phase of the battle, in the engagement near the Persian ships,[97] in which the general Stesileos and Aeschylus' brother Cynegeiros also met their death. During the battle Callimachus commanded the right flank of the Athenian array. This was consistent with prevailing tactics in Athens at that time, for the polemarch always had this position in battle and the men of each tribe were arrayed from right to left, according to the established order. The left flank was occupied by the 1000 Plataeans.

Callimachus was honoured immediately after his death with a votive offering to Athena on the Acropolis. This was a statue of Iris, messenger of the gods, set up on an Ionic column with capital. Between the flutes of the columns the ancient Greeks **15** incised an epigram, only fragments of which have survived. Its hypothetical completion[98] is based on the ancient metre and expressions in other epigrams or ancient texts.

[τένδε με δῆμος] ἔθεκεν ᾿Αφιδναίο[ν] τἀθεναίαι·
ἄν̣[γελον ἀθ]ανάτον, hοὶ ᾿Ο[λύμπια δόματα] ἔχοσιν.
[Καλίμαχος πολέ]μαρχος ᾿Αθεναίον τὸν ἀγõνα·
τὸν Μα[ραθõνι πρὸ h]ελένον ὀν̣[ομαστὸν ἔθεκεν·]
παισὶν ᾿Αθεναίον μν[ῆμα λιπὸν ἀρετῆς].

(This here, the messenger of the immortal gods who dwell on Olympus, the deme of the Aphidnians dedicated to Athena. The polemarch Callimachus made renowned the Athenians' struggle at Marathon for the salvation of the Greeks, and to the children of the Athenians left a monument of virtue).

47

Fig. 15a. Part of the column with Callimachus' epigram.

Fig. 15b (on the next page). A reconstruction of the monument of the Athenian polemarch.

The reading and completion of Callimachus' epigram on page 47 is one of several proposed by philologists and epigraphists. Five more readings and completions of the same text are given on the opposite page; all are based on strong arguments, but none is accepted unequivocally.

[Καλλίμαχος μ' ἀν]έθεκεν Ἀφιδναῖος τἀθεναίαι·
ἄν[γελον ἀθ]ανάτον, hοὶ Ὀ[λύμπια δόματ'] ἔχοσιν.
[Καλλίμαχος πολέ]μαρχος Ἀθεναίον τὸν ἀγõνα·
τὸν Μέ[δον τε καὶ h]ελένον ὅ[ρινε μέγιστον·]
παισὶν Ἀθεναίον Μα[ραθõνος ἀν' hιερὸν ἄλσος].
IG I² 609.   (1924)

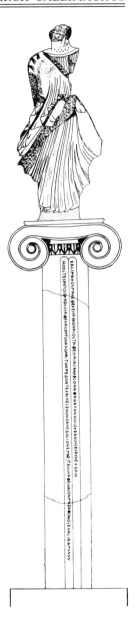

[Καλίμαχός μ' ἀν]έθεκεν Ἀφιδναῖο[ς] τἀθεναίαι·
ἄν[γελον ἀθ]ανάτον hοὶ Ὀ[λύμπια δόματ'] ἔχοσιν, /
[. . . .⁸. . . . πολέ]μαρχο[ς] Ἀθεναίον τὸν ἀγõνα·
τὸν Μα[ραθον. . . . h]ελενονο[. . . . .¹¹. . . . .·]
παισὶν Ἀθεναίον μν[. . . . . .²¹. . . . .]
Meiggs - Lewis, *SGDI* 18.   (1969)

[Καλίμαχός μ' ἀν]έθεκεν Ἀφιδναῖο[ς] τἀθεναίαι·
ἄν[γελον ἀθ]ανάτον hοὶ Ὀ[λύνπια δόματ'] ἔχοσιν.
[? Καλίμαχος πολέ]μαρχος Ἀθεναίον τὸν ἀγõνα·
τὸν Μα[ραθõνι πρὸ h]ελένον ὁ[(∪) – ∪∪̆ᶜᵃ·¹¹– – ·]
παισὶν Ἀθεναίον μν[εμ? – ∪∪̄–∪∪– –].
Hansen, *CEG* I 256.   (1983)

[. . . .⁹. . . . μ' ἀν]έθεκεν Ἀφιδναῖο[ς] τἀθεναίαι·
ἄν[γελον ἀθ]ανάτον, hοὶ Ὀ[λύμπια δόματ'] ἔχοσιν,
[ἐμέτερος πολέ]μαρχος Ἀθεναίον τὸν ἀγõνα·
τὸν Μα[ραθõνι πρὸ h]ελ(λ)ένον ὅ[νομ' ἐστεφάνοσεν·]
παισὶν Ἀθεναίον μν[έμεν δ' ἀρετẽς κατέλειπεν]
Hansen, *Hermes* 116, 1988, 482-483 [=*SEG* 38 (1988) 17]
                                                              (1988)

[? Καλίμαχός μ' ἀν]έθεκεν Ἀ<φ>ιδναῖο[ς] τἀθεναίαι· /
ἄν[γελον ἀθ]ανάτον hοὶ Ὀ[λύνπια δόματα] ἔχοσιν / *vacat*
[– ∪∪– πολέ]μαρχος Ἀθεναίον τὸν ἀγõνα· /
τὸν Μα[ραθον ∪∪] ΕⱢΕΝΟΝΟ [– – – –ᶜ·¹¹– – ·] /
παισὶν Ἀθεναίον μν[εμ – ∪∪̆ – ∪∪ – ∪̄].
IG I³ 784.   (1994)

49

Topography of Marathon

The Heracleion

The visitor to Marathon from Athens usually takes the road that passes through the modern villages of Pallini and Nea Makri. Just outside Nea Makri, near the American Base, is the area in which the most important sanctuary of Marathon was located, the temenos of Heracles mentioned by Herodotus in his description of the battle of 490 BC:[99] 'The Athenians were arrayed in the precinct of Heracles, and now the whole power of the Plataeans came to their aid'.

There are other testimonies to the existence of this sanctuary, namely two inscriptions that undoubtedly came from there. The subject of the earlier inscription,[100] slightly later than the battle of Marathon (490-480 BC), is the regulations for the games held in honour of Heracles (p. 137-138, no **21**).

The later one is an incomplete epigram,[101] dated after the middle of the fifth century BC, recording the dedication of some precious object to Heracles, perhaps for a victory in the Ἡράκλεια Ἐμπύλια (p. 138-139, no. **34**); because the Heracles worshipped at Marathon bore the epithet *Empylian*, that is he who is at the gates. It seems from the epigram that the narrow strip of dry land between Agrieliki and the sea, through which the traveller from the South had to pass, was known in antiquity, in the fifth century BC, as *Πύλαι* (gateway). This point, in the region nowadays known as Valaria, is the probable site of the highly revered sanctuary of Heracles.

The traveller Pausanias remarks that[102] 'The Marathonians worship both those who died in the fighting, calling them heroes, and secondly Marathon, from whom the parish derives the name, and then Heracles, saying that they were the first among the Greeks to acknowledge him as a god'.

We know of the games in honour of Heracles from the literary sources. They are mentioned by Pindar in the *Olympian Odes*[103] and the *Pythian Odes*.[104] According to the scholiast of Pindar, the poet says in the *Olympian Odes* that *'ἀργύρεαι φιάλαι ἆθλα ἦσαν ἐν Μαραθῶνι ἐν τοῖς Ἡρακλείοις'* (silver bowls (*ἀργυρίδεσσιν*) were the prizes in the Heracleia at Marathon).

Lucian[105] implies the Heracleion at Marathon when he writes that 'Herakles was established as a god but Eurystheus who commanded him had died. The temple of Heracles, who was a slave, and the tomb of Eurystheus, who was his master, lay close to one another'.

He refers to the story told by Strabo[106] of Eurystheus' campaign at Marathon: 'Now Eurystheus made an expedition to Marathon against Iolaus and the sons of Heracles, with the aid of the Athenians, as the story goes, and fell in the battle, and his body was buried at Gargettus, except his head, which was cut off by Iolaus, and was buried separately at Tricorynthus near the spring Macaria below the wagon-road. And the place is called ''Eurystheus' Head'' '.

From the testimonies of Lucian, who places the tomb of Eurystheus close to the temple of Heracles, and Strabo, who places it near the Makaria spring, another location for the Heracleion should be sought, in the northwest of the plain and not the southwest, in the area between Agrieliki and the sea.

According to the archaeologist G. Sotiriadis, the Heracleion was located very near the church of Saint Demetrios, in the **16** Vrana area. Some 100 m north of the church he had discovered a large precinct where, he claimed, the ephebes of Marathon exercised and were trained in the art of war. He maintained that the sanctuary of Heracles lay in this precinct.

Sotiriadis's opinion on the site of the Heracleion was also based on his conviction that the deme of Marathon was located thereabouts. On the top of the spur of Agrieliki towards Brexiza he had found an ancient enceinte, 300 m in perimeter, dating back to at least Mycenaean times. The houses would have stood on the lower reaches of the fortified rock.[107] However, neither finds nor recent examination of the ruins of the fortification have verified this view.[108]

The Makaria spring

Pausanias mentions the *Makaria* spring in his description[109] of the Marathon region: 'In Marathon is a spring called Macaria, with the following legend', which he proceeds to recount, finishing thus: 'Thereupon Macaria, daughter of Deianeira and Heracles, slew herself and gave to the Athenians victory in the war and to the spring her own name'.

The ancient Makaria is most probably the great spring (Megalo Mati) that still gushes forth at the side of the Bei-Kato Souli road, on the northeast edge of the plain, below Mount Stavrokoraki. Even now its abundant waters spill onto the plain, and once of a day it supplied Athens with water, as the

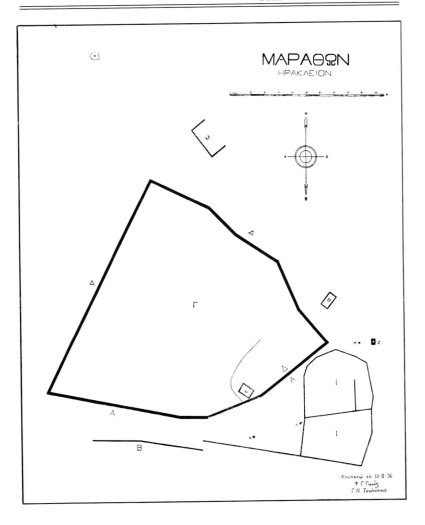

Fig. 16. Ancient enclosure near Saint Demetrios at Vrana, Marathon.

pumping station there attests. Indeed, during the German Occupation a guard was stationed by the spring and the small bunker for the soldier on duty has survived.

The waters of the Makaria spring traversed the plain, along a bed formed over the centuries, and flowed into a lake near Kynosoura. The lake is mentioned by Pausanias[110] straight after the Makaria: 'There is at Marathon a lake which for the most part is marshy. Into this ignorance of the roads made the barbarians fall in their flight, and it is said that this accident was the cause of their great losses'.

This marsh, the Megalo Helos, was drained in later times and indeed houses are now being built over its area. Part of it is still liable to flooding.

In ancient times the climate here was damp and probably unhealthy. Aristophanes[111] mentions the mosquitoes at Tricorynthos in his phrase ἐμπὶς Τρικορυσία (i.e. Trikorynthian mosquito). The scholiast of Aristophanes explains this: λέγεται ἐμπὶς Τρικορυσία ὡς ἐν Τρικορύνθῳ πολλῶν ἐμπίδων γινομένων, ἔστι γὰρ ἀλσώδης καὶ κάθυγρος ὁ τόπος (it is called Tricorynthian mosquito because there are many mosquitoes at Tricorynthos; the place is densely vegetated and very damp). Simonides[112] had this terrain in mind when he named the battlefield Μαραθώνιον ἄλσος, a phrase used much later by Pausanias,[113] Μαραθῶνι ἄλσος (the grove at Marathon). The traveller continues[114] that: 'Above the lake are the stone stables of Artaphernes' horses, and marks of his tent on the rocks. Out of the lake flows a river, affording near the lake itself water suitable for cattle, but near its mouth it becomes salt and full of sea fish'.

The belief in the stone stables of Artaphernes' horses is later and it seems that cuts from quarrying above the lake were considered to be these installations on account of their shape. Because the water issuing from the Makaria flowed unseen as far as the lake and thence into the sea, Pausanias regarded the lake as the source of fresh water, whereas it was only a juncture on the course of the stream from the spring.

Plasi

Some scholars locate the deme of Marathon at the site of Plasi, where traces of settlement from all periods —from Neolithic to Roman— have been found. In addition to Neolithic, **17** Early Helladic, Middle Helladic and Mycenaean pottery, an Archaic *peribolos* (enclosure) of monumental construction, indicates the continuous habitation, which was favoured by the coastal situation, the fertile soil and a water source. However, no evidence has yet come to light that would permit identification of the site with the nucleus of the deme, that is some sanctuary or inscriptions or *ex-votos*.[115]

In other demes, neighbouring Rhamnus for example, the settlement proper has been found, with houses, streets, small sanctuaries, workshops and so on. Here at Plasi there are no characteristic remains of a centre of a wealthy deme such as Marathon. Perhaps the ancient Marathonians lived in farmsteads dispersed throughout its territory, as was clearly the case in later times.

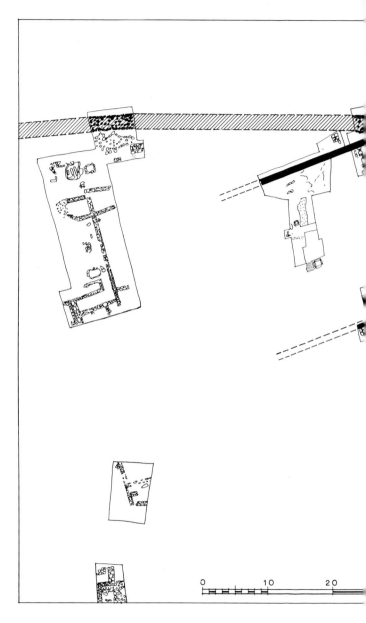

Fig. 17. Prehistoric building remains at Plasi, Marathon.

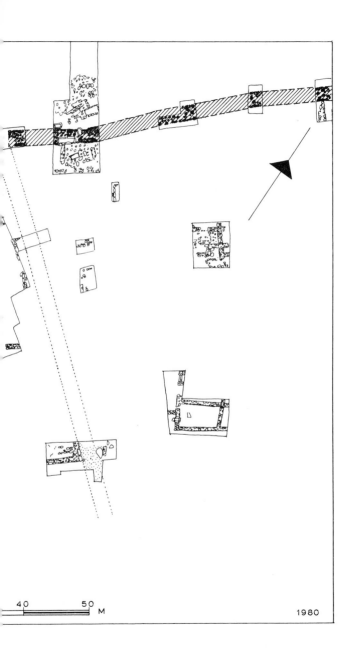

40   50 M

1980

Tsepi

The major prehistoric centres systematically investigated at Marathon are the Early Helladic cemetery at Tsepi and the Middle Helladic one at Vrana. The site of Tsepi lies on the 18 edge of the plain, at the base of the little Mount Kotroni, the summit of which has been made into a military helicopter pad.

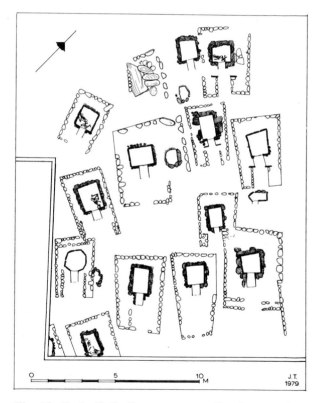

Fig. 18. Early Helladic cemetery at Tsepi, Marathon.

There Sp. Marinatos excavated[116] a large Early Helladic cemetery in which the graves are arranged in orderly rows. The rectangular or circular graves were lined inside with slabs or rubble walling and were provided with an entrance at the front blocked by stones. Large slabs were used as capstones and then covered with earth. The corpse was inhumed in contracted pose. When the grave was to be used anew the bones of the previous burial were collected together in order to make room for the next. From the construction of the graves and the few grave goods recovered from them it is deduced this cemetery was used by inhabitants of the Cyclades who had settled on the east coast of Attica, perhaps to engage in trade.

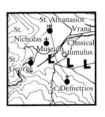

Vrana

A short distance from the site of Tsepi, to the southwest, stands the Marathon Museum, built in close proximity to the Middle Helladic cemetery at Vrana, in the foothills of Mount Agrieliki. Comprising seven burial mounds, four of which were **19** investigated by Sp. Marinatos,[117] this is one of the most important cemeteries in Attica. These tumuli were known in the nineteenth century and were briefly described by Leake and Fraser. Surrounded by stone slabs in circular arrangement, they are shield-shaped, attaining a maximum height of 1.50 m above the surrounding flat land. In the interior of the tumuli there is a second circular construction and at least one shaft grave that was covered by slabs. The dead were buried in contracted pose.

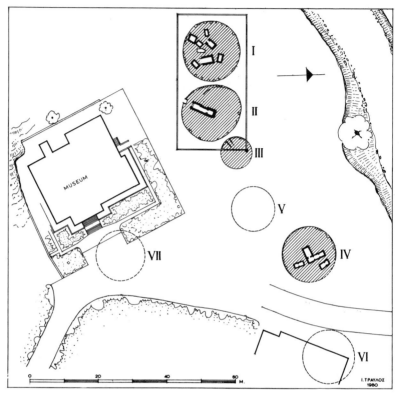

Fig. 19. Topographical plan of the Marathon Museum and the tumuli at Vrana.

The tumuli were used over a long period of time. Tumulus I contained seven cist or shaft graves, one in the inner circle and the rest between the inner and the outer circle. Tumulus II is of irregular circular shape with a grave at the centre surrounded by three internal enclosures. Tumulus III, small in

60

area, contained two built shaft graves. Tumulus IV, large and **20**
virtually circular, diam. 15 m, was destroyed by the installation
of an Italian gun emplacement during World War II. The
main feature of the interior is the long narrow space partitioned
by small walls into four sections full of mixed up bones, a few
small vases and spindle whorls. Marinatos ascertained that the
bones came from those cleared and collected to created space,
and not from dead who had been buried there from the outset.

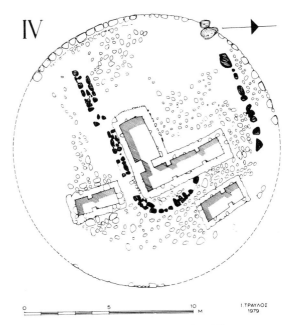

Fig. 20. Grave tumulus IV at Vrana.

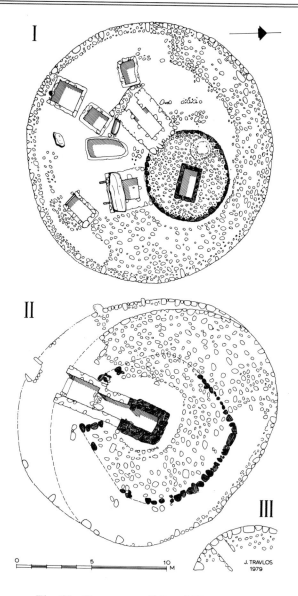

Fig. 21. Grave tumuli I and II at Vrana.

Tumulus I dates from the Middle Helladic period (2000-1600 BC), II is a generation later and, according to Marinatos, **21** dates after 1550 BC, while the finds from the other two tumuli are later and date to the fourteenth and thirteenth centuries BC.

The tholos tomb

Four hundred metres southeast of the tumuli cemetery stands a complete Mycenaean tholos tomb, internal height 7.20 m, restored and roofed. It was investigated in 1933-1935 by **22** Georgios Sotiriadis,[118] the excavator of Thermos, Ephor of Antiquities and subsequent university professor.

The tomb's interior, 7 m in diameter, contained two shaft graves in each of which a gold vase, a cup or beaker, was found. At the beginning of the 25 m-long, sloping passage (*dromos*) leading to the tomb the skeletons of two horses were found, on their side and confronting each other. According to I. **23** Papadimitriou, who investigated[119] the burial in 1958, these horses were offered to the dead, just as in the heroic age immortalized in the lines of the *Iliad*[120] in the description of the cremation of Patrocles, which was followed by games and the awarding of prizes by Achilles.

The tholos and the mouth of the tomb are of well-built, dry-stone walling and the entrance is crowned by a large, monolithic lintel, above which is a relieving triangle. The large monument was restored[121] in 1958.

The tholos tomb at Marathon, a rare funerary monument in Attica (there are other tholos tombs at Menidi and Thori-

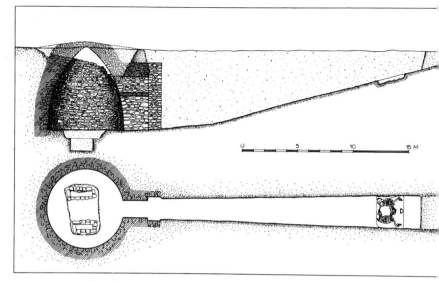

Fig. 22. Mycenaean tholos tomb at Arnos, Marathon.

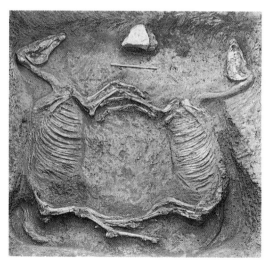

Fig. 23. Two horse skeletons at the beginning of the dromos of the Mycenaean tholos tomb at Marathon.

kos), is dated to 1450-1380 BC. In his excavation report, Sotiriadis says that the tholos was full of bones and charcoal, indicating that sacrifices were made to the heroized dead in the tomb. In Marinatos's opinion[122] this constitutes a final shift from the tumuli to the tholos tomb of rendering divine honours to the dead in the Mycenaean era.

The Classical tumulus

Not far to the east of the prehistoric tumuli cemetery at Vrana, Sp. Marinatos partially explored[123] a mound over 3 m **24** high and 30 m in diameter. Eleven burials were found, two of which were cremations, that is the dead had been burnt to ashes. All the dead were male, including a boy of about 10 years old.

Over the burials, which Marinatos considered as contemporary, a large pyre had been lit, sacrifices offered to the dead and vases deposited as grave goods. A large stone slab had been set upright on top of each inhumation as a funerary stele. Sometime later, according to Marinatos, a tumulus composed entirely of river pebbles was raised over the graves.

The grave goods were Attic black-figure vases dated between 500 and 490 BC: lekythoi, plates,[124] handleless cups, a black-glaze pyxis and a black-figure loutrophoros.

The fact that all the dead were men, in conjunction with the date and contemporaneity of the burial, led Marinatos to propose that this tumulus was that of the Plataeans who fell in the battle of Marathon. He suggested that the ten year old boy

Fig. 24. Classical tumulus, known as that of the Plataeans.

was probably a messenger who brought the commands of the generals to the various ranks of warriors during the battle.

On the narrow side of the stele on one of the graves, of a man aged 30-40 years, the name 'Αρχία or 'Αρχία[ς] had been incised with a knife or a javelin. Marinatos assumed that Archias was an officer.[125]

The burial of the Plataeans on the field of battle is recorded by Pausanias:[126] 'On the plain is the grave of the Athenians, and upon it are slabs giving the names of the killed according to their tribes; and there is another grave for the Boeotian Plataeans and for the slaves, for the slaves fought then for the first time by the side of their masters'.

Automatically the same doubt is created for the tumulus of

the Plataeans as there was for that of the Athenians. Pausanias would not have called the mound we see τάφος (grave) but γῆς χῶμα (mound), as he does in other cases where he describes tumuli. A strong argument against Marinatos's claim is that the stele of Archias is written in the Attic alphabet and not the Boeotian, as would be expected if the inscription had been incised by a Plataean.

The sanctuary of Athena

East of the church of Saint Demetrios, in the foothills of Mount Agrieliki, G. Sotiriadis placed[127] the *Heracleion* (sanctuary of Heracles), where the Athenians had encamped in 490 BC. A few hundred metres away a marble boundary stone[128] was found, bearing the inscription *hόρος / τεμένος / 'Aθενάας* (boundary of the temenos of Athena). On investigating the find spot and its environs, Sotiriadis discovered a stele base, rooms of a small house and a pil-

25

Fig. 25. Boundary stone of the sanctuary of Athena.

67

lar-like pedestal with dedicatory inscription of the early fourth century BC, which is displayed in the Museum. From these finds and his study of the topography, E. Vanderpool concluded[129] that the deme of Marathon lay in the foothills of Agrieliki, in the southwest part of the plain of Marathon.

Mikro Helos - Nisi

In antiquity Mikro Helos (Small Marsh) was the southernmost territorial limit of the deme of Marathon. It was dried out in 1933 with the construction of a canal that drained the water into the sea. The project was financed by the American millionaire Rockefeller and the people of Nea Makri offered their labour. The former aspect of the landscape, today totally disfigured by buildings and embankments, is known from early **26** travellers and topographers.

The mire, fed by water issuing from the eastern foothills of Mount Agrieliki, spread out as far as the sea. A small area, approximately 100×150 m, projecting from its seaward edge, formed an islet, known as Nisi (Island) by the locals, around which ran a channel full of water emptying into the sea. When the outlet of the channel was blocked by sand deposited by the waves, the water level rose and Mikro Helos flooded more. In later times causeways gave access to Nisi from the surrounding mainland, as described by the French consul[130] in Athens Fauvel (1753-1838), agent and supplier of antiquities to the French Ambassador to the Sublime Porte, Choiseul-Gouffier: 'A small stream transforms the graves into an island and flows into the sea. A paved road joined the graves to the mountains, crossing the marsh. There is also a man-made causeway from the island in the sea which is 50 feet away'.

The graves referred to by Fauvel as belonging to the Athenians who fell in the battle of 490 BC, were ruins of ancient buildings. In his plan of the region (prepared in 1792), now in the Bibliothèque Nationale in Paris, he specifies the ruins he saw.

The supposed graves of the Athenians are in fact the ruins **27** of the temple of the Egyptian gods, while the busts of the emperors Lucius Verus and Marcus Aurelius, which Fauvel mentions, were found northeast of the balneum built by Herodes Atticus, as is noted on the plan of Nisi.

Fauvel shows the channel that virtually surrounded Nisi and marks in the west, above the paved road, a spring that supplied Mikro Helos, the existence of which was ascertained by Sotiriadis too.

Other travellers, apart from Fauvel, also describe the host of impressive antiquities visible in the region of Nisi. Excavations have brought to light a temple of the Egyptian gods and a balneum, both are described below.

Sotiriadis believed that Brexiza was the harbour of Marathon. According to the local people of his day, an ancient quay was preserved on the shore, and he himself had noted[131] the existence of a man-made canal of Roman date, which led in from the sea, penetrating the marsh. He described it as very wide, with sides protected by strong walls, and of dual function: it collected the water of the marsh and served as a haven for the fishermen's boats.

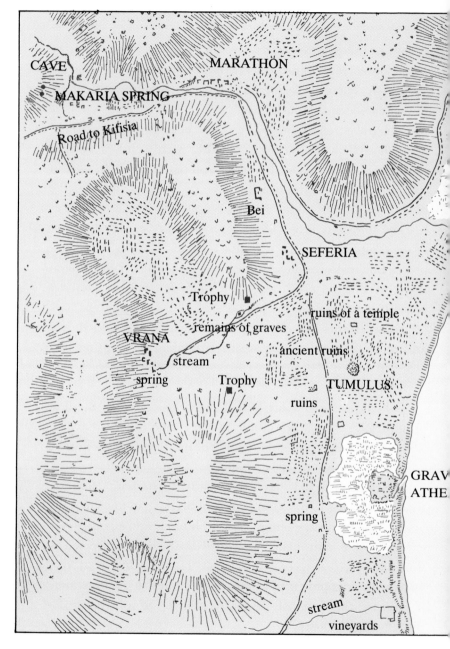

Fig. 26. Map of Marathon, after that drawn by Fauvel in 1792.

| 0 | | | 500 | | 1000 toises |
| 0 | | | 974.5 M. | | 1949 M. |

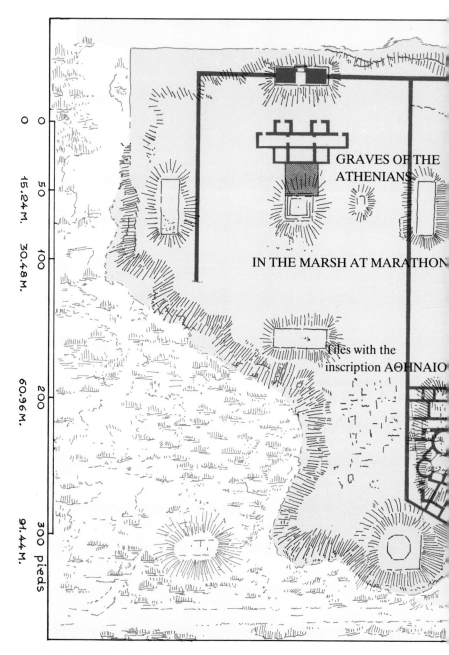

GRAVES OF THE
ATHENIANS

IN THE MARSH AT MARATHON

Tiles with the
inscription ΑΘΗΝΑΙΟ

0

0

15.24 M.

30.48 M.

50

100

60.96 M.

200

91.44 M.

300

pieds

Fig. 27. Map of Mikro Helos, after that drawn by Fauvel in 1792.

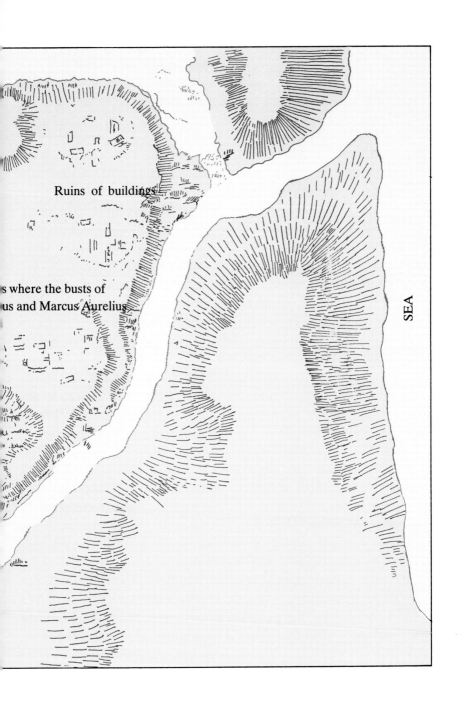

Ruins of buildings

s where the busts of
us and Marcus Aurelius

SEA

The sanctuary of the Egyptian gods

Directly north of the American base lie the ruins of two large ancient buildings of the second century AD; a sanctuary of an Egyptian deity and a bath installation (balneum). Both monuments are difficult to visit and to study on account of the dense, wetland vegetation that thrives thereabouts. Despite efforts to keep the site free, the copious waters of Mikro Helos create ideal conditions for the lush plant growth.

The sanctuary of the Egyptian gods[132] included a precinct wall 1 m thick, of which the section in which the propylon (width 2.40 m) stood is preserved. The propylon, with three steps and the threshold of the doorway, was of monumental, fortified aspect. The opening was flanked right and left by a solid, almost square (5.75 × 5.50 m) tower marking the terminus of the enclosure. Since it is built of unworked stones, bricks and lime plaster it is possible that the exterior was revetted with marble slabs, a common practice in Roman times.

On the outside of the propylon, left and right of the entrance, stood four larger than life size statues in the Egyptian style. One, 2.40 m high, represents Hadrian's favourite Antinoos in frontal pose, and can be seen in gallery V of the Marathon Museum. Only the lower part of the second statue has survived, on display in the same museum. This belongs to a female figure, generally assumed to be Isis on account of her attire. A third statue, intact and similar to the first, also representing Antinoos, is now in the National Archaeological Museum, Athens (Egyptian Collection no. 1). It was found at Marathon in 1843 and there is no doubt that its provenance was this sanctuary. The fourth statue has either been destroyed or is

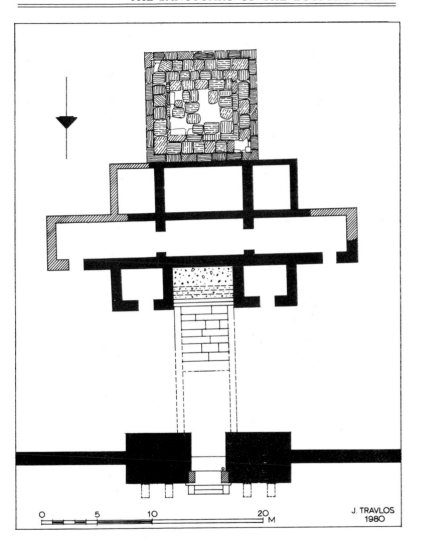

Fig. 28. Entrance to the sanctuary of the Egyptian god Kanobos at Mikro Helos, Marathon.

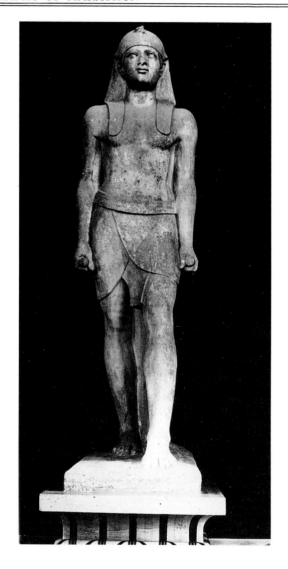

Fig. 29. Egyptian-style statue of Antinoos.

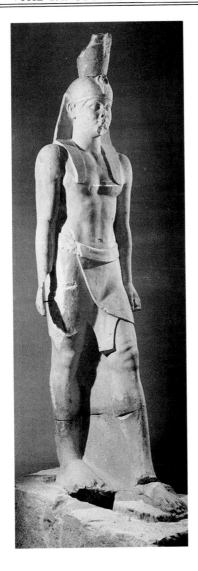

Fig. 30. Egyptian-style statue of Antinoos.

Fig. 31. Lower half of an Egyptian-style female statue.

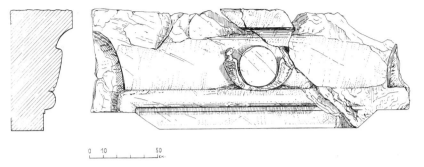

0 10   50
                 cm.

Fig. 32. Lintel of the entrance to the sanctuary of the Egyptian god Kanobos (drawing Manolia Skouloudi).

still concealed in the muddy ground of the sanctuary's environs. It is possible that the female statue and the missing one represented persons from the imperial circle of Rome.

The portal of the propylon had a marble lintel carved in relief with a solar disc encircled by a snake, possibly the Egyptian cobra, known as the *uraeus* in Egypt, the *basilisk* of the ancient Greeks. **32**

A paved street, 5.40 m wide, led from the entrance to the temple, only the shelly limestone foundations of which are preserved (9.70 × 10 m). Between the street and the temple is a building complex of six rooms. An oblong room in the middle with two entrances on its north side, two more or less square rooms with an entrance from the north, that mark the end of the paved road, and four rectangular ones between the oblong one and the temple.

The entire north side of the precinct wall of the sanctuary has survived in ruins. Half-way along is the monumental propylon previously described. The area enclosed by the *peribolos* extends a long way to the south but has not been investigated.

It is not known to which Egyptian deity the temple was dedicated. Its attribution to the cult of Isis, based on the bottom half of the female statue found in excavation, is completely arbitrary. There is a testimony in Philostratus[133] to the existence at Marathon of a sanctuary to the Egyptian god Kanobos, in whose temple the meeting was arranged between Herodes and Agathion, nicknamed the Heracles of Marathon. Philostratus[134] relates that this 'Heracles', a young man as tall as a Celt, was described by Herodes in one of his letters; apart from his magnificent physique, he wore wolf skins, was wont to wrestle with boars, jackals, wolves and wild bulls, and showed off the wounds he incurred in combat with such beasts. He was said to be born of the earth ($\gamma\eta\gamma\varepsilon\nu\grave{\eta}\varsigma$) of Boeotia. Herodes had heard him say that his mother was a cowherdess and his father Marathon, a farmer hero, to whom there was the statue at Marathon at that time.

Herodes admired Agathion and on one occasion invited him to dine with him; the 'Heracles' replied 'tomorrow I shall meet you at noon in the sanctuary of Kanobos'. There is no evidence of a second Egyptian sanctuary at Marathon, which would in any case be excessive. So the anonymous sanctuary at Brexiza, which, as we have said, has been attributed to Isis on account of the lower half of a female statue with the diacritica of this goddess, must be the sanctuary of Kanobos to which Philostratus refers. Kanobos, captain of Menelaus' flagship when the King of Sparta returned from Troy, died from a snake bite in Egypt and was buried there.

The building of a temple of the Egyptian gods may have been prompted by a possible journey to Egypt by Herodes or by a desire to imitate Hadrian, who had constructed a copy of the canal and the Serapion of Kanobos in his villa at Tivoli.

The canal spoken of above not only had a practical use but also constituted part of the Egyptian staging of the sanctuary. One side of it, the south, would demarcate the sacred precinct, which was thus accessible by boat. The other, the north, now lies under the nearby modern hotel.

The area of Brexiza with its abundant water, the island (Nisi) in the middle of the marsh, the proximity of the sea, the wide canal along which small boats could pass, are all features appropriate to the worship of Egyptian deities. The cult of Isis included rites associated with seafaring. Thus it is reasonable to believe that in the sanctuary at Marathon Kanobos was worshipped along with other Egyptian gods.

The balneum

The east side of the precinct of the sanctuary of the Egyptian gods, the seaward, is also preserved for a length of 90 m. **33-34** At its end, outside the sanctuary, a large bath installation, a balneum, has been revealed. This is a complex with several rooms for hot baths, not unlike the Turkish baths still operating in many parts of Greece.[135]

Bath houses were used in ancient Greece from very early times. The best known is the balneum at Olympia, the original form of which dates back to the fifth century BC. Its construction there was necessary to serve the host of pilgrims who gathered at the sanctuary. Balnei were public baths in which hot water and certain cosmetic services were available. They were also places where improprieties were not unusual, as Epic-

81

Fig. 33. Aerial photograph of the balneum at Brexiza.

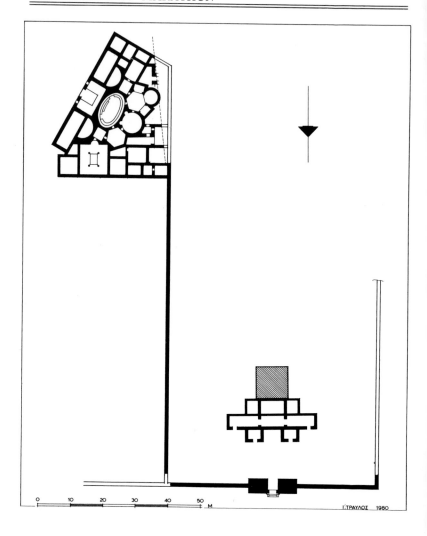

Fig. 34. Topographical plan of the sanctuary of the Egyptian god Kanobos and the balneum at Mikro Helos, Marathon.

tetus[136] pithily remarks in his *Encheiridion*: 'If you are going to bathe, think about the things that happen in the balneum, those who throw water on you, who push you, who curse you, the thieves'.

The entrance to the balneum was on the east side. At the centre of the complex there was a large elliptical chamber-pool, revetted in varicoloured marble. Here the cold baths were taken, while there were other facilities for the hot ones, as well as for the necessary preparation. In the ruined complex uncovered in excavation we see low pillars of brick preserved on the floor in certain areas. These are the so-called hypocausts. The pillars held up the real floor, below which steam circulated in pipes. Steam, which induced perspiration and so contributed to the cleansing of the skin, was produced in other ways too, the most common being to pour water onto stones heated in the fire.

The luxury of the building, its propinquity to the sanctuary of the Egyptian gods and the period in which it was constructed (second century AD) are the main reasons why the balneum is attributed to the generosity of Herodes Atticus, who had also paid for the sculpting of the busts of Lucius Verus and Marcus Aurelius, as well as of the portrait of himself which was found by Fauvel.

The Cave of Pan

The Athenians honoured the Arcadian god Pan for his help in the battle of Marathon, consistent with the promise he made to Philippides, as recorded by Herodotus:[137] 'Why is it that ye take no thought for me, that am your friend, and ere now have oft been serviceable to you, and will be so again?'.

The inhabitants of the Tetrapolis established the god's cult in a cave in the area of Oinoe. The traveller Pausanias describes[138] it briefly: 'A little beyond the plain is the Hill of Pan and a remarkable Cave of Pan. The entrance to it is narrow, but farther in are chambers and baths and the so-called "Pan's herd of goats", which are rocks shaped in most respects like to goats'.

The cave, evidently known in the nineteenth century, was **35** rediscovered in 1958 some 3 km west of the present village of Marathon, on the slope of the acropolis of Oinoe, on the south bank of the Charadra, the river that flows from its source on the north flanks of Penteli —present day Kokkinovracho— into the gulf of Marathon.

Partially explored in 1958 by I. Papadimitriou,[139] the cave has two entrances, the main one being the eastern. The ground outside it is flat and there are niches in the rock for votive offerings. A stele found beside this entrance is inscribed with a sacred law which will be discussed below. The cave is divided by stalactites and stalagmites into chambers, Pausanias' οἴκους (chambers), the small basins filled with water are the baths (λουτρά), and the pendent stalactites give the impression of a huddled herd of goats (πέτραι τὰ πολλὰ αἰξὶν εἰκασμέναι).

Use of the cave dates back to remote antiquity. Neolithic pottery and skeletons from burials of the same period were found there, a clay 'slingstone', stone axes and outstanding intact vases with painted or impressed decoration. Inside one vase were hundreds of necklace beads of blue glass paste and rock crystal, two stone axes and five small sea shells of the kind still worn as amulets by small children.

The prehistoric finds from the cave continued down to the

Fig. 35. Interior of the Cave of Pan at Oinoe.

end of Mycenaean times. I. Papadimitriou observed that these are confined to the chambers directly behind the entrance. It seems that after Late Helladic III the cave was abandoned and only begun to be used again after the battle of Marathon. In the historical era traces of the cult of Pan are numerous and continuous: terracotta figurines of Pan, goddesses and nymphs,

lamps, essential in the darkness of the cave, gold jewellery, At-
36 tic red-figure pottery.

Fig. 36a. Lamps from the Cave of Pan.

The worship of Pan and the Nymphs in the cave was formal
and organized, as a small stele found beside the east entrance
37 attests. This stele[140] was a dedication to the deities of the cave
from ephebes of 61/60 BC, as its text reveals: *'Αγαθῆ τύχη· ἐπὶ
Θεο/φήμου ἄρχοντος· / Πυθαγόρας καὶ Σωσι/κράτης καὶ Λύ-
σανδρος / οἱ συνέφηβοι Πανὶ καὶ / Νύμφαις ἀνέθηκαν. <α> /
ἀπαγορεύει ὁ θεὸς μὴ / [ε]ἰσφέρειν χρωμάτιν[ον] / [μ]ηδὲ βα-
πτὸν μηδὲ --*. Below the text of the stele there was probably a
relief of Pan and the Nymphs. Here the ephebes, young men
aged 18-19 years, give official notification of an interdiction not
properly observed by faithful pilgrims who offered indiscrimin-
ately to the god garments that were not to his liking, that is

Fig. 36b. Classical finds from the Cave of Pan.

Fig. 37. Sacred law of 61 BC, dedication of the ephebes to Pan.

coloured or dyed. The adorant should offer a white himation, an observance encountered at other sanctuaries too.

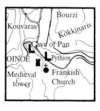

The Pythion at Oinoe

The existence of a sanctuary of Apollo Pythios in the region of the deme of Oinoe is attested by the commentary on lines 1047-1048 of Sophocles' tragedy *Oedipus at Colonus* (ἢ πρὸς Πυθίαις, ἢ λαμπάσιν ἀκταῖς, i.e. now to the Pythian shrine, now to the hallowed sand, where the bright torches shine). The scholiast explains that the poet 'calls Pythian shores the altar of Apollo Pythios that is at Marathon. From there the official delegation set forth for Delphi'. Philochorus, a third century BC expert on Attica, specifies the position of the altar of Apollo. The aforementioned scholiast cites a passage from his work the *Tetrapolis*: 'the seer sacrifices daily at the Pythion of Oinoe, when the procession for Delphi is being prepared and the theoria is sent. If, however, the theoria is sent to Delos, then, in accordance with what has been said, the seer sacrifices in the Delion at Marathon. And haruspication takes places (divination by inspecting the entrails of the sacrificed animal) in the Pythion at Oinoe for the theoria that is sent to Delphi, and in the Delion at Marathon for the theoria that is sent to Delos'.

In 1972, very close the medieval tower at Oinoe, Sp. Marinatos[141] investigated a large building comprising a rectangular peristyle 13.60 × 17.30 m. The marble pillars are square, of side 0.70-0.72 m, and stand on a marble stylobate of good workmanship, 0.92 m wide. On the inside of the peristyle, behind each pillar, is a block of marble 2.50 m long, 0.55 m wide and 0.87 m high. The upper surface is slightly hollow, of depth 0.065 to 0.095 m. On the inner edge of the blocks the surface is flat, of width 0.22 m, and bears two dowel holes. Travlos suggested that the dowels were used to affix another piece of marble as a bolster of these large blocks which will have been used as couches. **38** **39**

The narrow spaces (1.20 m wide) between the couches are blocked with marble parapets to the same height, 0.88 m, placed at a distance of 0.79 m from the pillars. These parapets, 0.072-0.085 m thick, were fixed in the cuttings made in the sides of the couches. Initially the constructors of the building

Fig. 38. The medieval tower at Oinoe.

had placed them at a distance of 1.16 m from the pillars, as the preserved cuttings indicate, but subsequently changed their
40 mind, cutting new grooves and blocking the first with bricks and lime that were coated with fine stucco. The floor between the pillars and the parapets is laid with marble slabs. A small, brick step revetted with imitation marble facilitated getting onto the couch. The floor of the interior of the building is 0.12 m higher than the stylobate of the pillars. Made of brick cement coated with lime, it is 0.14 m thick.

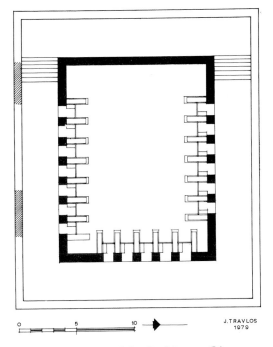

Fig. 39. Plan of the Pythion at Oinoe.

Since excavation of the building is incomplete no definite conclusions can be drawn concerning its purpose. The use of brick cement and the workmanship of the marble indicate that the peristyle with couches most probably dates to the time of Herodes Atticus, who seems to have been the motive force behind it. I. Travlos considered it to be an *enkoimeterion* (building for incubation), which he associated with the Pythion described by the scholiast of Sophocles and Philochorus, a very convincing opinion.

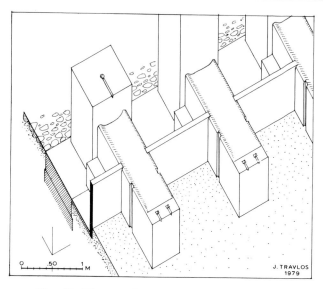

Fig. 40. The couches in the Pythion at Oinoe.

Incised on a section of pillar is the inscription *ΘΑ / 'Αλκία*. The letters *ΘΑ* perhaps stand for 'to the immortal gods' (*Θεοῖς*
42 *ἀθανάτοις*), while Herodes Atticus' mother is known to have been called Alkia. Full investigation of the monument should shed light on its precise purpose and its connection with Herodes.

Twenty-three metres west of the peristyle and virtually on
41 its axis are the foundations of a semicircular exedra 10 m in diameter.

The Delion spoken of by Philochorus was located in the environs of Marathon and should be sought closer to the sea.

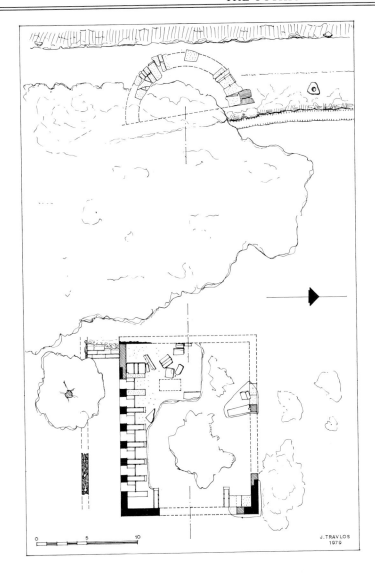

Fig. 41. Topographical plan of the Pythion at Oinoe.

Fig. 42. Alkia, inscription on a pillar in the Pythion.

Mythology of Marathon

In ancient times four cities occupied the wider region of present-day Marathon, forming a union originally known as the *Hyttenia*. It was later named the *Tetrapolis* (Four cities), which has the same meaning. The four cities (*Marathon, Oinoe, Trikorynthos* and *Probalinthos*) were founded by Xouthos, son of Deucalion, who had taken to wife the daughter of Erechtheus. Although all the cities of Attica submitted to the rule of Theseus, the institution of the Tetrapolis of Marathon was maintained in Classical times, as indicated by the inscriptions; the name Hyttenia survived in the worship of *Hyttenios*.

Heracles is linked with this region. The Marathonians were the first to regard him as a god and he was even depicted in the wall-painting of the battle of Marathon in the Poikile Stoa. The worship of Heracles was official and important, and his sanctuary, the Heracleion, is the key to the ancient topography of Marathon, for it was there, as we have seen, that the Athenians encamped in September 490 BC. Associated with Heracles are the local myths of Marathon, of Eurystheus (*Εὐρυσθέως κεφαλὴ*) and of the Makaria spring, thus named after the homonymous daughter of Heracles and Deianeira. However, the Attic hero *par excellence*, Theseus, is linked with the main myth of Marathon. According to the ancient authors and mythographers, when Theseus reached Athens from Troezen and was entertained in the house of his father Aegeus, still unknown, Aegeus' wife Medea guessed his true identity. In order to be rid of him she sent him to exterminate the monstrous bull that was destroying the crops on the Marathon plain. The bull was thought to be that of Crete, which Heracles had brought to

Fig. 43. Theseus and the Marathonian bull, on a metope of the Athenian Treasury at Delphi.

98

the Peloponnese. The mythographer Apollodorus[142] relates: '*πλανηθεὶς εἰς Σπάρτην τε καὶ Ἀρκαδίαν ἅπασαν, καὶ διαβὰς* **43** *τὸν Ἰσθμόν, εἰς Μαραθῶνα τῆς Ἀττικῆς ἀφικόμενος τοὺς ἐγχωρίους διελυμαίνετο*' (after it had roamed in Sparta and throughout Arcadia and crossed the Isthmus, it reached Marathon in Attica where it destroyed the local people). The bull snorted fire through its nostrils. Theseus captured it and sacrificed it to Apollo Delphinios.

Several versions of the myth exist, varying in the details. On the death of his father Aegeus, Theseus became King of Attica and achieved the *synoecism*, that is he united the many petty polities of the region into a single state with Athens as capital, seat of the Prytaneion and the Boule.

Other gods and heroes are associated with Marathon. Athena is mentioned in the *Odyssey*:[143] '*ἵκετο δ᾽ ἐς Μαραθῶνα καὶ εὐρυάγυιαν Ἀθήνην*' (on leaving Scheria 'She came to Marathon and broad-wayed Athens'). She was worshipped at Marathon with the eponym *Hellotis*, from *Helos* (marsh), in the lore of the ancient Greeks.

The mythology of Marathon is rich and varied, and the deities and heroes known from inscriptions are numerous. The few mentioned here have been chosen to explain the names associated with the ancient topography.

Herodes Atticus at Marathon

His life

Herodes Atticus, whose full name was Lucius Vibullius Hipparchus Tiberius Claudius Atticus Herodes, was born at Marathon in AD 103 and died there in AD 179.[144]

Thanks to his abilities and his teachers, Herodes distinguished himself as the pre-eminent sophist (orator) of his day. He studied with the famous Faborinus, a sophist from Arelate (Arles) in Gaul and the equally renowned Polemon, of whom two bombastic speeches concerning the battle of Marathon have survived, *Εἰς Κυναίγειρον καὶ Καλλίμαχον*. Pupils of Herodes included the orator Aelius Aristides (AD 129-189) and the Roman emperors Lucius Verus (AD 161-169) and Marcus Aurelius (AD 161-180). Herodes' relations with Rome were excellent, despite Marcus Aurelius' ephemeral dislike of him. In AD 143 Herodes was elected consul. In previous years he had exercised the duties of *agoranomos* (overseer of the market) in Athens, and in AD 126/7 had served as eponymous archon of that city.

Herodes inherited an enormous fortune from his father, which he used to finance public works and buildings. The Panathenaic stadium and the odeum that bears his name were constructed in Athens at his expense, the aqueduct at Olympia, the stadium at Delphi, the Peirene fountain at Corinth. He had a villa in Kynouria and his residences at Kephisia and Marathon were legendary. In addition to the sculptures and inscriptions from these, a host of his *ex-votos* —portraits of himself, of members of his family, of his pupils and of the Roman emperors— have been found, mainly in Athens and Attica, in the Peloponnese and in Euboea.

Herodes owes his reputation not only to his wealth and generosity, but also to his intellectual achievements. His speeches were 'in the tradition of a rhetoric that tried to keep the link with philosophy' (A. Lesky). He was very careful of his style, attaining an archaic purism which was so successful that one of his extant orations, *Περὶ πολιτείας*, was considered to be a work of the fifth century BC.

His estate

Herodes Atticus' homeland was Marathon. According to his biographer Philostratus, this, together with Kephisia, was where he loved to live in Attica, and it was here that he died. Though had left instructions that he be buried at Marathon, the Athenian ephebes brought his corpse to Athens and Herodes was laid to rest in the Panathenaic stadium.

He had financed impressive building projects at Marathon, such as the balneum and the sanctuary of the Egyptian gods, already discussed. To the northwest, in the area of Oinoe, is the so-called *Mandra tes Grias* (The Old Woman's Sheepfold), a **44** stone enclosure of rubble masonry 3,300 m in perimeter, which surrounded the country estate Herodes gave to his wife Regilla.[145] The property included various buildings and installa-

Fig. 44. Part of the Mandra tes Grias, Herodes Atticus' country estate.

tions, and in all probability Herodes' residence. The monumental entrance to the estate comprised an arched gateway with
45 inscriptions on the top of both faces. Incised on the outside
was:[146]

> Ὁμονοίας ἀθανάτ[ου]
> πύλη
> Ἡρώδου ὁ χῶρος
> εἰς ὃν εἰσέρχε[ι].

102

Fig. 45. Earlier reconstruction of the gateway to the estate.

(Gateway of Immortal Harmony. The place you enter belongs to Herodes).

The same inscription was incised on the inside,[147] with the difference that Ἡρώδου was replaced by Ῥηγίλλης, that is the name of his wife. In front of each external jamb of the gateway was a statue seated on an elaborate throne, the remains of which are in the Marathon Museum. Indeed the existence of a third statue is attested. About 1.70 m up the right jamb of the

46

47

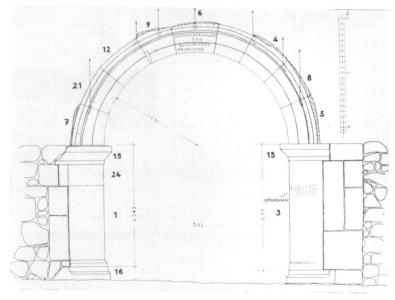

Fig. 46. Later reconstruction of the gateway to the estate.

gateway is the following epigram,[148] referring to Herodes and his wife Regilla:

ᵀΑ μάκαρ ὅστις ἔδειμε νέην πόλιν,
οὔν[ο]μα δ᾽ αὐτὴν
῾Ρηγίλλης καλέων, ζώει ἀγαλλόμενος.

Ζώω δ᾽ ἀχ[ν]ύμενος τό μοι οἰκία ταῦτα τέτυκται
νόσφ[ι] φίλης ἀλόχου καὶ δόμος ἠμιτελής.
ὣς ἄρα τοι θνητοῖσι θεοὶ βιοτὴν κεράσαντ[ες]
χά[ρ]ματα τ᾽ ἠδ᾽ ἀνίας γείτονας ἀμφὶς ἔχω.

104

In the first three lines of the epigram the unknown composer expresses his admiration of the happiness and greatness of the man who built the 'new city' that he beholds: 'O happy is he who built a new city, naming it after Regilla; his life is full of joy'.

In the following lines is the reply of the sad Herodes who has lost his wife. His bereavement occurred in AD 160 or 161, so the epigram was incised after that date:

'My life is full of sorrow as I contemplate my existence without my beloved wife, and my house that has remained without heir.

Truly, when the gods mix the mortals' cup of life they put in joys and sorrows mingled'.

Herodes' residence at Marathon must have stood in the area enclosed by the *Mandra tes Grias*, in which ancient build-

Fig. 47. The statues from the gateway to the estate.

ings —bath installations— have been haphazardly investigated. On this estate, then densely planted with olive groves and orchards, with vegetable gardens and with pastures where the livestock could graze, the cultured sophist lived in the luxury to which he was accustomed.

His ex-votos

Herodes' dynamic presence at Marathon is attested by finds from excavations there, even from the time of Fauvel. The sophist's most usual dedication was a herm bearing a portrait of himself or of one of his pupils. Such stelae have been found in all those parts of Greece with which Herodes is known to have been associated. His biographer Philostratus[149] (2nd-3rd century AD) writes of his three favourite pupils, Achilles, Polydeukes and Memnon: *'οὓς ἴσα γνησίοις ἐπένθησε τροφίμους ὄντας, ἐπειδὴ καλοὶ μάλιστα καὶ ἀγαθοὶ ἦσαν γενναῖοί τε καὶ φιλομαθεῖς καὶ τῇ παρ' αὐτῷ τροφῇ πρέποντες. εἰκόνας γοῦν ἀνετίθει σφῶν θηρώντων καὶ τεθηρακότων καὶ θηρασόντων τὰς μὲν ἐν δρυμοῖς, τὰς δὲ ἐπ' ἀγροῖς, τὰς δὲ πρὸς πηγαῖς, τὰς δὲ ὑπὸ σκιαῖς πλατάνων, οὐκ ἀφανῶς — οὓς οὐκ ἂν ἐπὶ τοσοῦτον ἦρεν, εἰ μὴ ἐπαίνων ἀξίους ἐγίγνωσκεν'* (whom he mourned, being his pupils, as his own children, for they were honest, kind-hearted, of noble disposition, eager to learn and honoured the upbringing they received in his home. So he dedicated their portraits, representing them hunting or after the hunt, or while preparing for the hunt, some in woods, some in fields, some beside springs, some in the shade of plane trees, always conspicuous —he would not have honoured them so much if he had not known that they deserved his praises).

Of these portraits of his pupils several headless and incomplete herms have survived, which can be attributed to each **48** thanks to the preserved inscriptions. They are usually accom-

Fig. 48. Bust of Polydeukion, from Kephisia.

107

panied by an imprecation too, of identical type in all, something encountered elsewhere too, at Rhamnus and Kephisia for example.

A pedestal[150] found not far from Pyrgos, in what were then vineyards, bears witness to an *ex-voto* of Polydeukion to Dionysos:

$$[\Pi]ολυδε[υκίων]$$
$$τῷ \ Διονύσῳ \ [εὐ]-$$
$$σεβξίας \ ἕνεκα.$$

(Polydeukion dedicated (it) to the god Dionysos because of his piety).

This was set up before the death of Herodes' beloved pupil, which took place in AD 173/174. On the contrary, the herm from Kato Souli, in ancient Trikorynthos, found incorporated in the wall of a well, dates from after his death. On its face are two inscriptions, the dedication[151] and the curse that protected Herodes' votive offering. The first inscription is the following:

$$Πολυδευ-$$
$$κίωνα, \ ὃν \ ἀν-$$
$$3 \quad ϑ' \ υ[ἱ]οῦ \ ἔστε-$$
$$(ρξ)εν \ καὶ \ ἐνϑά-$$
$$δε \ ῾Ηρώδης \ (ἀν)-$$
$$6 \quad έϑηκεν \ ὅτι \ ἐν-$$
$$ϑάδε \ καὶ \ περὶ$$
$$ϑήραν \ εἶχον.$$

(Here too Herodes dedicated Polydeukion, whom he loved as a son, because here too they hunted together).

Herodes' mother, Vibullia Alkia, had also set up a statue of Polydeukion amidst the orchards and vineyards somewhere in the Vrana region. Its base with the inscription,[152] now lost, is known from the nineteenth-century publication of it.

[Οὐιβού]λλιον Πολυδ[ευκίωνα]
[Οὐιβου]λλία ᾽Αλκία ῾Ηρ[ώδου μήτηρ]
[ἥρωα].

Two incomplete herms of Herodes' second pupil, Achilles, are known. The first was found west of the village of Varnavas, built into the wall of the church of the Virgin, and bears a brief dedicatory inscription:[153]

῾Ηρώδης ᾽Αχιλλεῖ·
ὃς βλέπειν σε ἔχοιμι
3 καὶ ἐν τούτω τῶ
νάπει· αὐτός τε
καὶ εἴ τις γ᾽ ἕτερος,
6 κἀκεῖνοί [γ᾽, ἔ]σπ με-
μνημένο[ς τῆ]ς ἡ-
μετέρας φιλίας ὅ-
9 σπ ἡμεῖν ἐγένετο·
ἱερόν δέ σε ῾Ερμοῦ ἐ-
φόρου καὶ νομίου
12 ποιοῦμαι.

(Herodes to Achilles; in order to see you I put you in this wood; I myself and anyone else, and all will remember how great was our friendship; I make you a dedication to Hermes the overseer and pastor).

The second herm,[154] found at Oinoe, close to the medieval tower, bears the inscription ᾽Αχιλλεὺς and a 29-line impreca- **49-50** tion with which Herodes protected it.

Herodes' third pupil was Memnon, an Ethiopian according **51** to Philostratus:[155] ῾Μέμνονα τὸν ῾Ηρώδου τοῦ σοφιστοῦ τρό- φιμον, ἀπ᾽ Αἰθιόπων δὲ ἦν᾽ (Memnon pupil of Herodes the so-

Fig. 49. Headless herm of Herodes' pupil Achilles, with interdictory curse.

Fig. 50. The inscription on the herm.

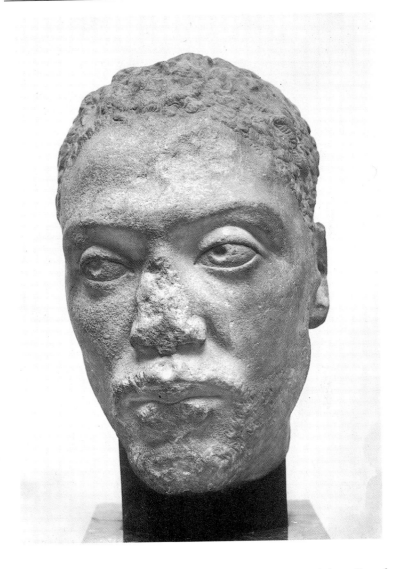

Fig. 51. Head of an Ethiopian, said to be Memnon (phot. Staatl. Mus. zu Berlin, no. 5588).

111

Fig. 52. Headless herm of Herodes' pupil Memnon.

phist was from Ethiopia). Two herms of Memnon have been found, one in the vicinity of the Mesosporitissa church and the second at Marathon, near Skorpio Potami. Both[156] bear the same dedicatory inscription:

Μέμνων,	Memnon,
τοπάδειν,	a small topaz,
Ἀρτέμιδος φίλος.	beloved by Artemis.

The word τοπάδειν, the interpretation of which perplexed epigraphists for years, means a small topaz,[157] a semi-precious stone. This was a pet name for Memnon, perhaps on account of his colour. A head of an Ethiopian, now in Berlin, is believed to

52

come from a statue of him, as is a hand of black marble, found
several years ago in Kephisia along with busts of Herodes and
Polydeukion.[158] The mention of Artemis alludes to Memnon's
hunting activities.

Herodes' exuberance in honouring his pupils did not please
all the Athenians. The sophist had rivals who caused him ser-
ious harm, manifesting their enmity in secondary issues too.
Popular reaction to the herms was expressed in damaging
them, and Herodes was obliged to incise new inscriptions on
those already standing. As Philostratus relates[159] in his brief
account of the incident, Herodes dedicated the stelae ξὺν ἀραῖς
τοῦ περικόψαντος ἢ κινήσοντος (accompanied by curses against
he who would break them or move them). So the incising of
curses was evidently a response to bad feeling against Herodes
and vandalism of his dedications.[160] The aforementioned herm
of Polydeukion bears an incised curse (*IG* II² 13190) with
which Herodes thought he could protect it from the hostile in-
tentions of the countryfolk. The first part is as follows:

> [Π]ρὸς θεῶ[ν καὶ ἡρώω]ν ὅ[στις]
> [εἴ ὁ ἔ]χων [τὸν χῶρον], μήπο[τε μετ]-
> ακεινήσ[ῃς τούτω]ν τ[ι· καὶ τὰς τ]-
> ούτω[ν τῶν ἀγαλμάτων εἰκόν]-
> 5 ας κα[ὶ τειμὰς ὅστις ἢ καθέλοι ἢ]
> μετακεινοίη, [τούτῳ μήτε γῆν κ]-
> αρπὸν [φέρειν μήτε θάλασσαν πλ]-
> [ω]τὴ[ν εἶναι, κακῶς τε ἀπολέ]-
> σθαι αὐτο[ὺς κ]α[ὶ γένος. ὅστις δὲ]
> 10 κατὰ χώ[ραν φυλάττοι καὶ τειμῶν]
> [τ]ὰ εἰωθό[τ]α [καὶ αὔξων διαμέ]-
> [ν]οι, πολ[λὰ καὶ ἀγαθὰ εἶναι τ]-
> [ούτ]ῳ κα[ὶ] αὐ[τῷ καὶ ἐκγόνοι]-
> [ς]

(In the name of the gods and heroes; whoever you may be master of the place, never move any of these here; and whoever takes down or moves these portraits and ornaments, may his earth bear no fruit, nor his sea be navigable and may he and his line be destroyed in a terrible way. But whoever leaves them in their place and cares for them and maintains them as appropriate, may he and his descendants see many good things).

There were also objections from the authorities. In the years when Herodes honoured his pupils, the Quintilii brothers from Alexandria in the Troad were governors of Achaea (Greece). Both Sextus Quintilius Condianus, vice-consul, and Sextus Quintilius Velerius Maximus, *legatus* or *corrector*, enjoyed the favour of Rome and both disliked Herodes.[161] They had no qualms about showing their disapproval of his numerous votive offerings, and according to Philotratus:[162] 'Κυντιλίων δέ, ὁπότε ἦρχον τῆς Ἑλλάδος, αἰτιωμένων αὐτὸν ἐπὶ ταῖς τῶν μειρακίων τούτων εἰκόσιν ὡς περιτταῖς "τί δὲ ὑμῖν", ἔφη "διενήνοχεν, εἰ ἐγὼ τοῖς ἐμοῖς ἐμπαίζω λιθαρίοις;"' (When the Quintilii, in the period they governed Greece, rebuked him for these portraits of young men, that is that they were excessive, he replied "What does it matter to you if I have fun with my little marbles?").

Fauvel, who has been mentioned before, was particularly active at Marathon. In October 1788 he excavated a tumulus on the plain, which he considered to be of the Athenians, without finding anything. He persisted in his efforts further south, in the Brexiza marsh, where he most probably investigated the sanctuary of the Egyptian gods. On 18 February 1789 some 53 villagers from Marathon in his employ brought him the bust of the emperor Lucius Verus, which had been found 'in the ruins of the grave of the Athenians', that is in the sanctuary of the Egyptian gods. Over the next two months Fauvel explored the 54-55 same area again, discovering the busts of the emperor Marcus

Fig. 53. Bust of the emperor Lucius Verus, from Brexiza (Ashmolean Museum, Oxford).

Fig. 54. Bust of the emperor Marcus Aurelius, from Brexiza (Musée du Louvre, Paris).

Fig. 55. Bust of Herodes Atticus, from Brexiza (Musée du Louvre, Paris).

117

Aurelius and Herodes Atticus. These last are now in the Louvre in Paris, while the bust of Lucius Verus is in the Ashmolean Museum, Oxford. All three were *ex-votos* of Herodes, who at about the same time dedicated the portraits of the same persons —the two emperors and himself— in the sanctuary of Nemesis at Rhamnus, a few kilometres further north.

Herodes mainly lived and taught in Athens, Kephisia and Marathon. Indeed Philostratus[163] narrates that after his return from Paeonia (Pannonia, a land south of the river Danube, in what is now Hungary, Yugoslavia and Austria): 'διῃτᾶτο μὲν ὁ Ἡρώδης ἐν τῇ Ἀττικῇ περὶ τοὺς φιλτάτους ἑαυτῷ δήμους Μαραθῶνα καὶ Κηφισιάν' (he spent his time in his favourite demes of Marathon and Kephisia). When at one time the sophist Alexander, surnamed Πηλοπλάτων (Mud-Plato), was passing through Athens and wanted to give lectures,[164] 'ἀκούων δὲ τὸν Ἡρώδην ἐν Μαραθῶνι διαιτώμενον καὶ τὴν νεότητα ἐπακολουθοῦσαν αὐτῷ πᾶσαν γράφει πρὸς αὐτὸν ἐπιστολὴν αἰτῶν τοὺς Ἕλληνας, καὶ ὁ Ἡρώδης "ἀφίξομαι" ἔφη "μετὰ τῶν Ἑλλήνων καὶ αὐτός" ' (on learning that Herodes was settled at Marathon and that all the young men had followed him there, he wrote him a letter asking for the Greeks, and Herodes replied "I shall come with the Greeks as well"). So when Herodes was present at Marathon it became a centre of philosophy and learning, to which the young men of Athens came in order to hear the mentor.

The Marathon Museum

T he Marathon Museum, situated on the site of the Vrana excavations at Marathon, near the Middle Helladic cemetery, was built at the expenses of the businessman and archaeophile Evgenios Panagopoulos. Inaugurated in July 1975, it houses antiquities from excavations in the wider region, exhibited in chronological order and, as far as possible, according to kind.

GALLERY I

Cave of Pan

This room is devoted almost exclusively to Neolithic pottery recovered from the Cave of Pan at Oinoe, discussed above. Neolithic installations have been explored in other parts of the Marathon region, primarily at Nea Makri, where the remains of a settlement have been found. The dwellings have been reconstructed graphically and light shed on many aspects of everyday life.

As is to be expected, the pottery from the Cave of Pan is better preserved, but as yet general information on the life of its Neolithic inhabitants is scant. Future excavation in the cave should fill in the gaps in our knowledge of this period, about which so much has been learnt in recent years as a result of systematic publication of Greek research.

CASE 1. Pottery of the Late Neolithic period (4000-3400 BC).

Top shelf: Matt-painted vases decorated with black linear motifs —bands, oblique lines, chevrons— on the light ground of the clay, typical of Late Neolithic pottery throughout mainland Greece. Here mainly sherds are displayed, since whole vases of this period rarely survive. Noteworthy are the broken leg of a rare, hollow figurine (**361**) and fragments of vases with bichrome decoration (**428, 1356**).

Middle shelf: Mainly vase sherds of the same matt-painted ware with linear decoration — panels, dentellated bands, zigzag lines, groups of bands, triangles, lozenges. Outstanding is the intact jug **1357** with globular belly. Most of its surface is undecorated, except for groups of three vertical lines, isolated or in pairs, linked by oblique, stepped lines, at opposite points. Fine horizontal bands on the rim.

Bottom shelf: Sherds of the Late Neolithic and Sub-Neolithic periods (4000-3200 BC), mainly of coarse-ware vessels and pithoi with incised motifs or plastic (relief) decoration imitating the rope with which such vases were actually bound at that time.

CASE 2. The pottery on the top and bottom shelves is later than that in Case 1, dating from the so-called Sub-Neolithic or Final Neolithic period (3400-3200 BC).

56

Fig. 56. Neolithic jug no. 1357, from the Cave of Pan.
Fig. 57. Deep bowl no. 641, from the Cave of Pan.

Top shelf: Pottery decorated with rectilinear patterns, symmetrically and asymmetrically placed, painted in lustrous red on the thick buff slip. This style is distinctive of Attica and is observed on Neolithic finds from the ancient Agora at Athens. The deep bowl (phiale) **641** with appliqués and vertical **57** pierced lugs midway up its height, probably used for suspension with string, is virtually intact. The red-painted decoration consists of vertical lines with triangles between. Noteworthy are the sherds with grooved decoration, characteristic of the period.

Middle shelf: Late Neolithic and Sub-Neolithic pottery from the Cave of Pan, with incised decoration of simple and stippled triangles, panels, zig-zag lines, stepped lines, successive chevrons surrounded by dots, lozenges. The vases with oblique mouth and large handles are regarded as ritual vessels. The imprint of a straw mat is preserved on the surface of vase **1332**.

Fig. 58. Globular vase no. 673 covered by vase no. 1396, from the Cave of Pan.

Bottom shelf: Fragments of so-called burnished ware, in which the surface of the vase has been carefully smoothed with a hard wooden or bone tool. The mottled surface on some sherds is due to imperfect firing.

CASE 3. Pottery of the Early Helladic I period (3200-2700 BC).

Top shelf: Fragments of domestic ware with handles of various shapes. No. **1444** has a tubular spout and others have relief ornaments imitating metal prototypes. Noteworthy is the closed globular vase **673** with cylindrical neck and two double pierced lugs. It was found in excavation covered by part of the lower section of vase **1396**, which is decorated with incised circles filled with dots. The vessels evidently belonged to a woman, since **673** contained a necklace of several hundred beads of blue glass-paste, coloured stone and rock crystal, two small stone celts and five sea shells of the kind still worn today as amulets by young children. Noteworthy is the black-ground pottery decorated in white (**1399, 1401, 1407**).

58

122

Middle shelf: Fragments of monochrome vases in black and bright red.

Bottom shelf: Fragments of vases with handle — vertical pierced lug (**1436**), cylindrical (**1437**), strap (**1449**). All indicate the variety of forms of handmade pottery in the Early Helladic period.

GALLERY II

Exhibited here are pottery and small finds from graves of the Early Cycladic period (3200-2000 BC) excavated at Tsepi a few hundred metres north of the Museum, from the Middle Helladic graves (2000-1600 BC) under the shelter adjacent to the Museum, and vases of the Geometric and Archaic periods, products of Attic workshops, found in tombs in the Marathon region.

CASE 4. Vases from the cemetery at Tsepi, Early Cycladic I (3200-2700 BC).

Top shelf: The most important exhibits are the two frying-pan vessels **58** and **74**, and the bowl (phiale) **39**. Several studies **59-60** have been made of the frying-pan vessels of the Cycladic period and diverse interpretations of their use proposed, none of which enjoys universal acceptance. No. **74** bears incised decoration on its lower surface. Around the circumference is a zone of dense parallel lines, followed by an inner zone of 9 clusters of concentric circles, interlinked by tangents, thus creating a running spiral pattern, a familiar theme in all periods of Greek art from

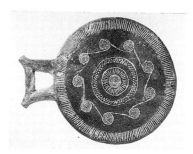

Fig. 59. Frying-pan vessel no. 58, from Tsepi.
Fig. 60. Cycladic frying-pan vessel no. 74, from Tsepi.

the Mycenaean until Late Antiquity. At the centre are concentric circles, small triangles and radiate lines. Frying-pan vessel **58** also bears incised decoration in circular arrangement of dense lines and tiny triangles, and at the centre a spiral with 15 radiate lines. Noteworthy too is the decoration of the bowl or **61** pyxis lid **39**, consisting of an incised four-point star at the centre of which is a smaller one inscribed in a circle. The design is enlivened by a second stippled line alongside each incised one. **62** The Cycladic bowl **73** bears an incised four-point star on the base and a rayed circle at the centre.

Middle shelf: Small vases, the majority globular in shape, closed, wide-mouthed, with incised linear decoration: vertical hatching at the base of the neck (**69**), line and dots (**658**), lines on the belly (**830**), zig-zag lines (**37, 647**), spirals (**53**).

Bottom shelf: Domestic vessels, undecorated and of various shapes; closed globular, conical bowls, a Cycladic jug,

Fig. 61. Cycladic bowl or pyxis lid no. 39, from Tsepi.
Fig. 62. Cycladic bowl no. 73, from Tsepi.

bowls. Noteworthy are the stone and bone tools, pestles, perhaps used for grinding pigments, and bone palettes.

CASE 5. Here too some of the numerous finds from the graves in the Early Cycladic cemetery at Tsepi (3200-2700 BC) are displayed.

Top shelf: Figurines, jewellery and small finds linked with everyday life. The three marble figurines (**298, 304, 453**) 63 schematically render the human figure; the head has no neck, the arms are triangular protuberances on the sides, the body rectangular. Figurine **454** is more developed, with a triangular head, long neck, and rudimentary indication of the trunk and legs.

Middle shelf: Assorted small domestic vases, fragments of silver bands used as adornments (**44** is gilded), a miniature axe (**29**), beads of steatite and of bronze, cores and blades of obsi-

Fig. 63. Cycladic figurine no. 304, from Tsepi.
Fig. 64. Globular vase no. 66, from Tsepi.
Fig. 65. Flint blade no. 586, from Nea Makri.

dian. The sole source of this hard, volcanic, glass-like stone is the Cycladic island of Melos. From the large pieces, the cores, fine long blades with serrated edges, used as knives or tools, were struck by skilful percussion.

Bottom shelf: The globular vase **66** dominates by virtue of its size: its height (0.18 m) is more or less equal to its diameter (0.192 m). It has a narrow, conical neck and two vertical, pierced suspension lugs. This was evidently no ordinary vessel, since the potter decorated it with dense, vertical plastic ribs, running from the base of the neck to the flat base, or slightly above.

As tends to be the norm with grave goods the vases here are intact. The shapes are repeated.

Fig. 66. Kantharos no. 3, from Vrana.

Noteworthy is the exceptionally large flint blade **586**, of **65** length 0.28 m, with serrated edges. It was found in an Early Helladic level at Nea Makri.

CASE 6. The vases and other grave goods are from the graves of the Middle Helladic (2000-1600 BC) and Late Helladic (1600-1100 BC) tumuli adjacent to the Museum.

Top shelf: The beak-spouted jugs are from tumulus I. No. **6** is undecorated, whereas **7** and **10** bear now faint matt-painted decoration of lines and triangles. The kantharoi are the distinctive vases of the Middle Helladic period. No. **3** is grey with the **66** characteristic horizontal grooves.

Middle shelf: The familiar vase shapes of the Middle Helladic period include the jug (**1**) and the kantharos (**4**). Other shapes are the biconical flask (**12**) and the Minyan ware pithoid vase with basket handle (**9**). The rock crystal bead (**458**), the obsidian, flint and bronze arrow heads, the small bronze knife

127

(**20**) and the stone spindle whorls (**2**) are all grave goods (*kter-ismata*). Also exhibited on the middle shelf are three Mycen-aean miniature vases (14th century BC), a one-handled cup (**20**) and two amphoriskoi (**15, 32**).

Bottom shelf: Most of the objects on this shelf date from the Mycenaean period (LH IIIA and B, 1400-1200 BC). The vase shapes are well known: stirrup jars (**29, 30**), alabastra (**26, 27**), small jug (**24**), kyathoi (**22, 25**), basin (**23**). There are numerous spindle whorls of clay, steatite and stone, as well as beads of faience and sardonyx.

Noteworthy are two Middle Helladic vases from the exca-vation at Plasi, a coastal settlement near Marathon. One (**700**) is a beak-spouted jug with matt-painted decoration of brown and red bands on the neck and an outline representation of a bird with its head turned right. The other (**701**), also a jug, is restored to a height of 0.21 m. Of its decoration a bird with outspread wings, painted in black and red, has survived.

These vases are particularly interesting because they are of Cycladic type, indicating contacts between Marathon and the Cyclades during the Middle Helladic period.

CASE 7. Many years ago, in 1934 and 1939, G. Sotiriadis, excava-ted a Geometric cemetery in the vicinity of the Mycenaean tholos tomb. The large number of vases recovered were in very good con-dition and the usual shapes of Attic Geometric pottery are repres-ented.

Top shelf: Lekythos **101** is decorated with a continuous zig-zag line and fine bands on only one section of the vase, the rest being covered with black paint. Oinochoe **836**, the same shape as a modern flask, is decorated with concentric zones on both sides: on one side these are of acute-angled triangles and zig-zag lines, on the other there are lozenges instead of triangles. At the centre is a white cross infilled with black lines. Oinochoe **842**, with twisted handled, is covered in decoration: on the neck, the shoulder and the belly is hatched meander pattern, in the intervening zones there are black bands, zig-zag lines or triangles.

The bird-shaped vase **846** stands on a low conical base and has an arched handle. One side is decorated with oblique parallel lines and the other with net pattern.

Middle shelf: Pyxides are a characteristic vase shape of the Geometric period. They are mainly decorated with meander pattern on the sides or metopes with swastika motif, four-petalled rosette or vertical zig-zag lines, as on examples **88, 123** and **193**. Of interest are the clay beads in a variety of shapes —spherical, biconical, cylindrical— decorated with incised or impressed circles, metopes or spirals.

Bottom shelf: Amphora **79** has two vertical handles on the neck and spare decoration. On the neck a square metope with four horizontal zig-zag lines defined by bands and small vertical lines, while the rest of the vase is covered by black zones interrupted by narrow black and light-coloured bands. This decoration is characteristic of early works and was usual in the mid-ninth century BC.

Pyxis **192**, is decorated with metopes with meander pattern, **67** swastika motif, circles, spirals. These same decorative themes can be seen on amphora **853**, along with meander, triangles **68** and clusters of lines.

CASE 8. The pottery exhibited here is contemporary with that in case 7 and comes from the richly furnished burials in the Geometric cemeteries of Marathon. The dominant vases in case 7 were the densely

Fig. 67. Geometric pyxis no. 192 from Skorpio Potami.

Fig. 68. Geometric amphora no. 853, from Skorpio Potami.

decorated pyxides. In case 8 the cups decorated with human figures or geometric ornaments have pride of place.

Top shelf: Tall cups with high-flung handle. Depicted on **134** is a dance of nine men holding sticks, between zones of triangles. On **107** are six women holding branches, on **125** swans in silhouette, lozenges and net pattern triangles. Painted on **117** are triangles and checker-board pattern. Kantharos **95**

69

Fig. 69. Geometric tall cup no. 107, from Skorpio Potami.

is decorated with three metopes, in the central one of which is checker-board motif and in the lateral ones birds. Represented on vase **82**, with its two, low-set handles, is a deer with antlers between two birds.

Middle shelf: The hydria **845**, larger than the norm, is decorated with lines, bands and a central metope filled with four clusters of inverted chevrons. Likewise unusually large is the spherical pyxis **143**, of which the curved lid with semicircular handle has survived. The decoration is purely geometric: meander, zig-zag line, lozenges, bands, triangles. The trefoil-mouth oinochoe **108** has two confronted birds, zig-zag lines and **70-71** four vertical wavy lines on the front. The same decoration is repeated on the back, except for the birds, while on each side there are five concentric circles with a star at the centre.

131

Figs 70-71. Geometric trefoil-mouth oinochoe no. 108, from the area south of Marathon.

Bottom shelf: The one-handled cups **145, 146, 148** are poor vases found in a child's grave at Marathon. The kalathos **135** is decorated with metopes with quatrefoil ornament and con-fronted birds, while the remaining vases, cup **147**, kyathoi **140** and **141**, and bowl (skyphos) **137**, have simpler decoration of zig-zag lines, dotted lozenges, bands or simply dark paint inside and out.

CASE 9. Displayed here is Archaic Attic pottery from graves in the Marathon region. More precisely, the vases cover the period from the second quarter of the sixth to the early fifth century BC. The majority are products of known, mediocre Attic workshops, such as that of the Polos Painter and of the Swan Group.

Top shelf: Preserved on the neck of the closed, black-figure vase **1456** is the representation of a woman flanked by two sphinxes. A sphinx and a cock are depicted on the shoulder of lekythos **460**, while on the belly of the vase is a winged figure running between two elderly men.

Though the black-figure choe **567** is largely restored, a warrior on horseback, facing right, is preserved. Depicted on the black-figure lekythos **678** are men and women moving right. Sphinxes, heraldic or in line, are the principal motif on the **72-73** black-figure plate **566**.

Middle shelf: Small, black-figure, nuptial lebes (**221**) decorated with confronted ducks and an imaginary beast with the head and mane of a lion and the body of a bird. Globular aryballos with ducks and rosettes (**729**). Fragment of a closed vase with zonal decoration (**1478**): in the first a lion facing right and in the second deer facing right.

Fragment of a vase with a cock on the belly (**1477**). Pyxis with representation of swans (**211**). Kothon with row of ducks (**730**). Kotyle with representation of confronted animals (**187**). Kotyle with representation of a bird in flight and two confronted lions (**465**).

Bottom shelf: Incomplete terracotta mask from Plasi (**281**). Figurine of a goddess seated on a throne (**105**). Clay pig figurine with traces of white pigment (**102**). Figurines **102** and **105** were found in a grave at Aghios Andreas. Two lekythoi (**262, 467**) of the same type (Deianeira) from graves in the Marathon region.

Figs 72-73. Black-figure plate no. 566.

GALLERY III

Trophy

The great battle fought in September 490 BC has already been discussed thoroughly. Here are exhibited some mementoes of it. Set up in the middle of the gallery is a section of an important monument in Athenian history, two drums and the Ionic capital of the column on which the Athenians erected the trophy of their resounding victory at Marathon, perhaps a statue of Nike. This trophy comprised a single, unfluted column with Ionic capital, on top of which stood a statue of Nike in flowing robes.[165] The capital was painted in vivid colours. The **74-75** design of the Ionic cymatium, egg and dart pattern, is still preserved on the echinus. Standing sentinel on what was at that

Fig. 74. The Ionic capital from the trophy; front face.

135

time the deserted plain, the monument symbolized Athens' struggle for freedom and the sacrifice of 192 of her sons, who remained there forever, under the earth of the mound raised over them. Plutarch[166] mentions this trophy in his *Life* of the admiral Themistocles: 'νέος ὢν ἔτι τῆς ἐν Μαραθῶνι μάχης πρὸς τοὺς βαρβάρους γενομένης καὶ τῆς Μιλτιάδου στρατηγίας διαβοηθείσης σύννους ὁρᾶσθαι τὰ πολλὰ πρὸς ἑαυτῷ καὶ τὰς νύκτας ἀγρυπνεῖν καὶ τοὺς πότους παραιτεῖσθαι τοὺς συνήθεις, καὶ λέγειν πρὸς τοὺς ἐρωτῶντας καὶ θαυμάζοντας τὴν περὶ τὸν βίον μεταβολήν, ὡς καθεύδειν αὐτὸν οὐκ ἐῴη τὸ τοῦ Μιλτιάδου τρόπαιον' (Even though he was a young man when the battle against the foreigners took place at Marathon and the general-

Fig. 75. The Ionic capital from the trophy; upper face.

ship of Miltiades was known to all, they saw him most of the time broody, awake at nights and having abandoned the usual drinking bouts, and saying to those who wondered and asked about this change in his life, that the trophy of Miltiades did not let him sleep).

The marble stele **19**, found east of the church of Saint Demetrios, not far from the Museum,[167] is the boundary stone of a sanctuary of Athena of the early fifth century BC as the majuscule inscription '*hόρος τεμένος ’Αθενάας*' (boundary of the temenos of Athena) indicates.

There are inscriptions on both sides of the other marble stele (**21**), h. 1.60 m. On one is a fragmentary text of the late **76** sixth century BC, probably related to the political and judicial reforms of Cleisthenes, after the fall of the Pisistratids at that time. On the other, incised in 490-480 BC, is a decision specifying the manner of election of the archons of the Heraclean games at Marathon,[168] a festival established after the battle of 490 BC.

> [Μ]αρ[αθōν]ι hερακλείο[ις τō]-
> [ν]αγōν[α] τιθέναι τὸς ἀ[θλοθ]-
> 3 έτας· τριάκοντα ἄνδρ[ας ἐς]
> τὸν ἀγōνα ἐπιόφσασθ[αι ἐκ]
> τōν ἐπιδέμομ, τρ̄ες ἐκ [φυλε̄]-
> 6 ς hεκάστες, hυποσχομ[ένος]
> ἐν τōι hιερōι ὃς ἂν οἷόν τ’ ε̄]-
> ι χσυνδιαθέσεν τὸν ἀ[γōνα,]
> 9 μὲ ὄλεζον ε̄ τριάκοντ[α ἔτε]
> γεγονότας· τούτος δὲ [τὸς ἄ]-
> νδρας ὀμόσαι ἐν τōι h[ιερō]-
> 12 ι καθ’ ἱερōν· ἐπιστατε̄[σαι δ]-
> [ε̄ - - -].

Fig. 76. Regulations for the conduct of the Heracleian games at Marathon.

(The Heracleian games at Marathon will be organized by the *agonothetes*; thirty men will be elected for the games, three from each tribe, from those who promised at the sanctuary to help as much as possible for the games to be held, they will be no younger than thirty years old; and these men shall swear an oath in the sanctuary, upon the holy sacrifices. Will officiate [- - - - - - - -]).

The metrical inscription **34**, from the Valaria area, is in-
77 cised on the face of the pedestal of an *ex-voto* dedicated to Heracles, in his sanctuary, and is dated to after the mid-fifth century BC. Preserved in the text is the epithet of the god ἐμ-

πύλιος, that is he who stands before the gates, implying that the sanctuary of Heracles was located beside the narrow passage between Mikro Helos at Marathon, on the seaward side, and Mount Agrieliki on the landward. This route was known to the ancient Greeks as *Pylai* (Gateway). The most probable reading and completion of the inscription on the base[169] is the following:

Ηρακλεῖ τόδ' ἄγαλμα τελεσ[- - - - - -]
τὸμπυλίοις ἀνέθεκε ηερακ[λείοισι- - -]

Fig. 77. Votive epigram of a victor in the Heracleian games at Marathon.

(This here is dedicated to Heracles, for his joy - - - for the victory at the Heracleia Empylia).

CASE 10. The room contains two cases with pottery. Exhibited in this one are vases found in the excavation of the Tumulus of the Athenians, conducted by Ephor Valerios Stais on behalf of the General Ephorate of Antiquities.

The majority are black-figure lekythoi with various representations and motifs, the usual grave good around the year 490 BC, while a few vases are outstanding by virtue of their quality or size.[170].

78 **Top shelf:** Black-figure tripod pyxis of the mid-sixth century BC (**764a**). On each leg a representation: a) Poseidon with trident in his raised left hand. On his right panoplied Athena mounting a quadriga. In front a clothed man. b) Goddess mounting a quadriga, before which is a seated man. On a second plane, Apollo playing the lyre; before him a female with raised arm. c) At the centre a male, possibly Apollo, playing the lyre; right and left two wreathed females facing the god and holding a flower in their raised right hand. Black-figure lekythos, work of the so-called Marathon Painter (**740**): Himation-clad Dionysos with red fillet on his head, mounts a quadriga. On a second plane, a Maenad with conical coiffure and a dancing female. Black-figure lekythos with artless representation of a kneeling female and an indeterminate figure (**758**). Black-figure lekythos (**750**): Athena battling with a giant, flanked by mounted Amazons. Black-figure lekythos with row of palmette ornaments (**754**). Black-figure lekythos, damaged and incomplete (**739**): Herakles brandishing his club, a lion, Athena and Hermes. Black-figure lekythos in poor condition (**737**): Hermes with caduceus and winged sandals, biga. On a second plane, a standing female with castanets. Dionysos and a female, perhaps

Fig. 78. Black-figure tripod pyxis no. 764a, from the Tumulus of the Athenians.

Ariadne, mount the chariot. Vase **738**: Theseus in combat with the Minotaur. Vase **741**: Two couples of Silens and Maenads dancing.

Middle shelf: Red-figure kylix (**848**): At the bottom a circle with black meander. The elbow and the feet of a figure running right are all that remain of the representation. Black-glaze pyxis, lid missing (**847**). Black-glaze skyphoid kylix (**764b**) with reserved band below the rim, inside and out. Plemmochoe-kothon with reddish-brown coat and traces of white paint (**763**). Large black-figure lopas (**766**): At the centre of the interior a rosette encircled by three broad, concentric bands. On the rim rosettes, on its side face vertical lines. On the exterior a **79** zone of boar and deer, with radiate foliate pattern below.

141

Fig. 79. Lopas no. 766, from the Tumulus of the Athenians.

Black-figure lekythos of the Marathon Painter (**755**): Satyr on quadriga, right, with satyr in front; Dionysos and Maenad behind. Black-figure lekythos (**749**), with parts of the human figures preserved. Black-figure lekythos with row of rosettes (**752**). Black-figure lekythos with two reclining males between two seated females (**759**). Black-figure lekythos with two youths on horseback (**745**). Black-figure lekythos preserving part of a quadriga (**751**). Black-figure lekythos (**756**): Three human figures dancing in front of a standing male. Black-figure lekythos with representation of Athena battling with a giant, flanked by two mounted figures (**757**). Black-figure lekythos with representation of Dionysos in a chariot and Silenus (**850**). Black-figure lekythoi decorated with row of palmettes (**760,**

753). Black-figure lekythos with representation of a chariot (**742**). Black-figure lekythos with representation of quadriga facing right and the charioteer (**744**). Black-figure lekythos with representation of quadriga facing right and human figures (**748**). Black-figure lekythos (**746**). Herakles attacking a beast (perhaps the Eurymanthian boar, as on **747**). Black-figure lekythos (**747**). Herakles attacking the Eurymanthian boar.

Bottom shelf: Black-figure hydria (**762a**). Metope on the front, between the horizontal handles: at the centre Dionysos, **80**

Fig. 80. Black-figure hydria no. 762a, from the Tumulus of the Athenians.

Figs 81-82. Cinerary urn no. 7626, from the Tumulus of the Athenians.

behind a billy goat. Left and right two satyrs, each bearing a maenad on the right shoulder. Black-figure lekythos (**849**): Horseman between two satyrs. Black-figure lekythos (**743**): Mounted warrior between two hoplites. Wide-mouthed globular vase with two high-flung, horizontal handles on the **81-82** shoulder and no neck (**762b**). It contained burnt bones. On the shoulder a row of hooks, on the rest of the body plain bands of unequal width. The shape is identified as the ancient *sipye*, a vase for the storage of barley flour or cereals.

Stais ventured the bold suggestion[171] that this vase contained the bones of a general, of Callimachus or Stesilaos, which view was accepted by Semni Karouzou, but cannot be proven. It is not an Attic vase, as Stais was the first to point out, and is perhaps of Eretrian provenance. The placement in it of the bones of one slain in the battle indicates that this indi-

144

vidual was treated differently from the other 191 victims. His identity, however, can only be guessed at.

In addition to the vases in case 10, the sherds of a black-figure amphora (EAM **1036**) were also recovered from the exca- **83** vation of the tumulus. A work of Sophilos, the first vase-painter known by name and whose heyday was the decade 580-570 BC, it is 0.635 m high. Depicted on the tall neck are two confronted sirens; between them is a palmette, above which stands a lion or a panther. Below are two heraldic sphinxes, separated by the god Hermes, standing and facing left. At the edges of this re-'presentation, a lion and a panther. Depicted on the other side of the neck is a siren above, flanked by a panther right and left, and two lions below separated by a composite palmette.

On the body of the vase very incomplete representations in zones: a) confronted lions, composite palmette and two sirens; on the other side Hermes with caduceus, goddess with sceptre, siren and panther. b) Two sitting sphinxes with composite palmette between, panther, boar; on the other side winged Artemis holding a lion by the tail in each hand. c) Two sirens, a panther and a swan; on the other side two confronted boar betwen a lion and a panther. d) Zone with ducks. A similar zone exists on the upper section of the vase on the exterior of the rim.

Some of the vases in case 10, the lekythoi **737-741**, are works of the so-called 'Marathon Painter', conventionally named from these very lekythoi. Some traits of these vases are observed on others, from elsewhere in Attica, which fact attests to the existence of an organized pottery workshop selling its wares throughout the region.

CASE 11. The black-figure pottery in this case dates from the early fifth century BC and comes from what is regarded as the tumulus of

Fig. 83. Black-figure amphora NAM no. 1036, painted by Sophilos, from the Tumulus of the Athenians.

146

the Plataeans who fell in the battle of 490 BC. Here too the lekythoi are numerous, though there are other vases as well, including plates and a loutrophoros.[172]

Top shelf: Black-glaze, handleless cups (kyathoi) with low foot (**158, 159**). Black-glaze kyathos (**154**). Black-figure plate of type A (**156**): Rim grooved on periphery, provided with two **84** suspension holes and painted with lotus garland. At the bottom a hoplite pursuing a fleeing hoplite. Plate **157** is very like **156**. **85** On the rim a myrtle wreath. At the bottom a Maenad facing right, with a dancing satyr on either side. Black-glaze skyphoid kylix (**155**).

Middle shelf: Handleless cup with black-glaze exterior (**164**). Small, black-glaze fruitstand (karpodoche) (**176**). Omphalos phiale (bossed bowl). Black-glaze interior (**162**). Omphalos phiale (bossed bowl) (**175**). Black-glaze kotyle (**161**). Miniature handleless kyathos with bands inside and out (**163**). Plate with strap handles and black bands inside and out (**851**). Lower half of black-figure lekythos; three figures on stools (**167**). Black-figure lekythos (**166**); two females in a chariot and another two alongside and in front of it. Lower half of black-figure lekythos; part of a male figure and an animal (**168**). Lower half of black-figure lekythos; two figures in quadriga and another two in front (**169**). Lower half of black-figure lekythos (**170**) with representation of reclining male. Two females left and right, leaving in opposite directions. Lower half of black-figure lekythos (**165**) with little of the representation preserved. Lower half of black-figure lekythos with little of the representation preserved (**171**). Lower half of black-figure lekythos (**172**): A chariot wheel, the leg of a figure and a male right are all that remain of the representation. Lower half of black-figure lekythos (**173**), showing the lower part of a figure.

Figs 84-85. Black-figure plates nos 156 and 157, from the Classical tumulus at Vrana.

Bottom shelf: Pyxis with lid (**174**). Black-glaze inside and **86** out. Black-figure loutrophoros with incomplete representations

Fig. 86. Black-figure loutrophoros no. 160, from the Classical tumulus at Vrana.

(**160**): On the neck two females holding wreaths. On the belly, front, a chariot facing right with two passengers. A figure in front of the chariot, next to it Apollo (part of his kithara has survived) and behind a nude male. On the back, three females with wreaths.

GALLERY IV

As the visitor can easily see, most of the exhibits in the Marathon Museum come from graves. They were the gifts (*kterismata*) with which the ancient Greeks honoured their dead. Exhibited in this room, in addition to the pottery in the showcase, are funerary sculptures of the fourth century BC, the era in which this art form in Attica attained its zenith, to disappear suddenly, without decline. A sumptuary law imposed by the ruler of Athens Demetrios of Phaleron (317-307 BC) banned the construction of luxurious sepulchral monuments and specified exactly what kind of grave markers the Athenians were entitled to set up on the tombs of their relatives, as well as the funeral rites they could perform. The sculpting of funerary stelae was forbidden, which explains the absence of these after 317 BC. For centuries there were no sculpted grave stelae in Attica; these reappeared at a later date. The monumental tombs were the so-called enclosures, large stone-built structures within which the dead of a family were buried. Remains of dismantled enclosures have been found at Marathon, in the locality Seferi, at Pyrgos and by the tower near the church of the Virgin Mesosporitissa. In the time of the Roman occupation the majority had already been demolished, and the destruction was completed under Frankish rule. Then the large, ashlar blocks of marble were considered ideal material for the building on the Marathon plain of the tall, majestic rectangular towers used as look-out posts and places of refuge from pirates. A third tower still stands, virtually intact, at Oinoe. However, the form of the fourth-century BC enclosures can be seen a few kilometres further north, at Rhamnus, where several have been restored.

The marble funerary lekythos **104** of the fourth century BC from Pallini does not bear a relief representation, as is usually the case, but preserves traces of painted decoration, floral motifs and meander pattern. We should imagine it brightly coloured, just as the funerary reliefs and stelae were painted in vivid blue, black, red and yellow.

The relief funerary stele **32** also dates to the fourth century **87** BC. On the right a woman seated on a stool, standing before her a maidservant with a folded cloth, a customary funerary offering of the ancient Greeks.[173] The typical expressions on the women's faces do not hide their sorrow. The seated figure is the deceased, one Phainarete according to the inscription on the architrave: *Φαιναρέτη Ν[ι]κίου Κεφαλῆθεν*. The stele was found at Kato Charvati (Pallini).

The relief representation on the marble lekythos **35**, of the first half of the fourth century BC, shows a seated female at the centre, greeting a male standing before her, while another female watches the scene.[174] The stele was found in the Vrana area of Marathon.

Stele **103**, of the fourth century BC, from the cemetery near **88** the Museum, bears a typical representation. A female seated left (*Pausimache* according to the inscription on the architrave) holds an open pyxis (jewellery casket) in her hands, while the female standing before her has another pyxis in her left hand.[175]

Fig. 87. Funerary stele no. 32, from Pallini.

Fig. 88. Funerary stele no. 103, from Vrana.

Fig. 89. Funerary stele no. 102, from Kato Souli.

The fourth-century BC funerary stele **102**, from Kato Souli, **89** is preserved in fragmentary condition. A female seated left hands to her maidservant, standing before her, a babe in swaddling bands. This is a rare scene of everyday life, with which the relatives who commissioned the stele wished to remember that the dead woman left behind her little orphan child.[176]

Pedestal **17** bore an *ex-voto*, probably a large relief, to an **90** unknown deity. The dedicatory inscription,[177] incised in handsome lettering of the early fourth century BC, reads:

Θεογένης Γύλητος Πρ-
οβαλίσιος ἀνέθηκεν
Ὀνητορίδης ἐπόησεν.

Fig. 90. Base with dedicatory inscription no. 17, from the Arnos region.

155

(Theogenes son of Gyles of Probalinthos dedicated (it). Oneto-rides made (it).

We shall come across this same Theogenes, from the neigh-bouring deme of Probalinthos, again on another monument in this gallery.

On the fourth-century BC funerary stele **14**, from Mara-
91 thon, is a nude young man standing right and leaning against a low column. At his feet is a hunting dog and in front of him a slave boy holding a strigil in one hand —an allusion to the dead youth's athletic activities— and a bird in the other. The theme of the young naked athlete is encountered on several Attic grave stelae of the fourth century BC, the most famous of which is the Ilissos stele in the National Archaeological Mu-seum, Athens. The Marathon stele continued above with another piece of marble bearing the head of the youth and the architrave of the relief.

Marble base **33** comes from the Plasi area; carved on its
92 façade is the following inscription[178] of the fourth century BC:

$$Οἵδε \ ἀνέθεσαν \ [ἐπὶ \ . \ . \ . \ .]$$
$$ωνος \ παιδοτριβοῦν[τος]$$

3	Μοσχίων	Κλεομέδ[-]
	Πείσων	[- - - - - - -]
	Οὐλιάδης	[- - - - - - -]

(Those mentioned below dedicated (it), when [- -]on was *paido-tribes* (gymnastic master). Moschion Kleomed[-] Pison [- -] Ou-liades [- -]).

These names are of the young men who had made financial contributions to the setting up of the *ex-voto*, a square herm. A special feature of the base is that on its upper surface, in front of the square cutting in which the herm was fixed, a bossed

Fig. 91. Funerary stele no. 14, from Marathon.

Fig. 92. Marble base no. 33, from Plasi.

bowl is carved, perhaps alluding to a victory in the Heracleian games.

The small statue of a naked child (**3**) comes from the sanc-
93 tuary of the Egyptian gods at Brexiza, where it had been used

158

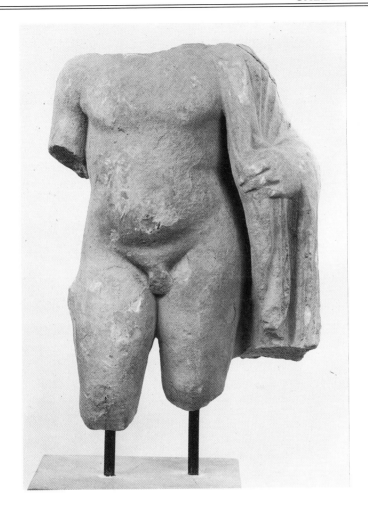

Fig. 93. Statue of a nude boy no. 3, from Brexiza.

as building material. The garment hanging from the left shoulder is held back by the boy's hand. This small statue of the fourth century BC is a usual votive offering in sanctuaries, particularly of healing deities.[179]

The two marble, Panathenaic grave amphorae of the second half of the fourth century BC, **30** and **31**, come from a family funerary monument. They are thus named because they copy the shape of the clay amphorae which, full of oil, were awarded to the victors in the Panathenaic games. These examples were found in an ancient cemetery near the Museum and stood on tombs of members of the family of Theogenes son of Gyles from Probalinthos, to whom base **17** belonged. The **94** relief representation on amphora **30**[180] includes five figures: a seated female greeting a man standing before her, another man in priest's robes holding the sacrificial knife, a little girl and, last, a second woman. Incised above the first two figures are their names: *Θρ[ασ]υβούλη, Γύλης Θ[εογένος]* (Thrasyboule, Gyles son of Theogenes).

The second marble Panathenaic amphora (**31**) is more **95** complete. Here too there are five figures, but they occupy different positions in the representation. They can be identified from the names incised above their heads.[181] First is a standing female, *Θρασυβούλη 'Ικαριόθεν* (Thrasyboule of Ikaria), and next to her a little girl leaning against the knees of the second, seated, female, *Φειδο[στρ]άτη* (Pheidostrate).

The males comprise a second group. First the priest with the sacrificial knife in his right hand *Θεογένης* (Theogenes), and before him his son *Γύλης Θεογένος Προβαλίσιος* (Gyles son of Theogenes of Probalinthos). From three monuments in the gallery, **17**, **30** and **31**, we learn that *Theogenes Gyletos* was a priest who had a son named *Gyles*, evidently a victor in the Panathenaic games. *Gyles* was married to *Thrasyboule* from

Fig. 94. Marble funerary panathenaic amphora no. 30, from Vrana.

161

Fig. 95. Marble funerary panathenaic amphora no. 31, from Vrana.

the Attic deme of Ikaria (present-day Dionysos), and his mother, Theogenes' wife, was Pheidostrate. The granddaughter **96** of Theogenes and Pheidostrate remains anonymous.

The marble statue of a female (**15**) in chiton and himation, holding a pyxis (jewellery casket) in both hands, is a funerary sculpture. The head was carved from another piece of marble. This late fourth-century BC work will have stood upon a grave, inside a marble naiskos.

CASE 12. Most of the vases displayed here are from the graves excavated at Aghios Andreas, between Rafina and Marathon. A few are from the area of Skorpio Potami, near the Museum. All the objects date from the first half of the fifth century BC and are run-of-the-mill products of pottery workshops.

Top shelf: Black-figure kylix (**230**) with zone of palmettes on the exterior. Black-figure lekythos (**214**) with two reclining figures. Black-figure skyphos (**234**) with double representation of chariots and charioteer between palmettes. Black-figure kylix (**205**) with Maenad inside, and Athena with shield and spear fighting three warriors outside. Black-figure kylix (**210**) with Maenad inside and a man struggling with a lion outside. Black-figure lekythos (**551**) with representation of a chariot. Black-figure kylix (**226**) with the same decoration as **230**.

Middle shelf: Black-glaze pyxis (**274**). Black-figure *hypo-staton* (**603**) with gorgoneion. Black-figure lekythos (**223**) with **97** sphinx atop a stele. Black-figure alabastron (**777**) with representation of a couple and a deer. Plate (**786**) with ray ornament on the inside, broad concentric bands and black discs on the rim, surrounded by dotted circles. Two broad bands on the outside.

Fig. 96. Funerary statue of a woman no. 15.

Fig. 97. Black-figure plate no. 786, from Skorpio Potami.

Plate **785** is the same as **786**, but the decoration is less well preserved. Black-figure alabastron (**574**) with two zones of net pattern. Noteworthy is the moulded vase **1482**, comprising two **98-99** like female heads attached to the back. They are separated by the intervening triangular section with checker-board pattern in black and white. The craftsman made both figures in the same mould but differentiated them by adding details. Vases of this type are rather rare. This piece was found in a grave at Skaleza, a site on the road to Oinoe.

Bottom shelf: Red-figure lekythos (**331**) with youth playing with two balls. Red-figure lekythos (**328**) with Cupid. Red-figure lekythos (**458**) with standing female. Lekythos (**541**) with lion. Red-figure loutrophoros (**810**) with females on the neck and belly.

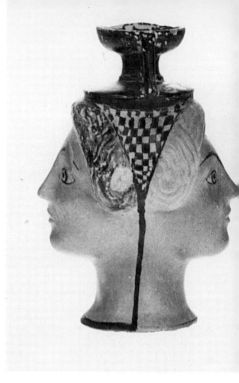

Figs 98-99. Moulded vase no. 1482, from Skaleza.

GALLERY V

Herodes Atticus

The last gallery in the Museum contains antiquities from the period of Roman rule in Greece. Dominant among them are two statues from the sanctuary of the Egyptian gods at Brexiza.

Of considerable historical interest is the metrical inscription **100 22**, incised on a stele crowned by a pediment with a shield at

Fig. 100. Stele no. 22 with the description of the Athenians' welcome of Herodes Atticus.

the centre. Though part of the text is missing, that which survives records[182] the glorious welcome the Athenians gave Herodes Atticus on his return to Athens, probably in AD 175, after a long absence due to litigation against him by his rivals. The Athenians, repentant of their bad behaviour and deprived of Herodes' generosity, rushed *en masse* to meet him on the Sacred Way, on the Thriasian Plain, at the point where the Rheitoi —spring streams— flowed into the sea. The intriguing inscription, compiled in the linguistic form of the Homeric epics, describes in detail the Athenians' arrival at the Rheitoi and the position of the various social groups that participated in the procession.

> Ὄλβιος, ὦ Μαραθών, νῦν ἔπλεο, καὶ μελεδαντὸς
> ἀνδράσιν ἠὲ πάρος, φαίδιμον Ἀλκαΐδην
> 3 νοστήσαντ᾽ ἐσορῶν ἀβίων ἀπὸ Σαυρομάταων
> γαίης ἐκ νεάτης, ἔνθα φιλοπτολέμῳ
> Αὐσονίων βασιλῆι συνέσπετο τῆλ᾽ ἐλάοντι.
> 6 Τὸν μὲν ὁ κισσοφόρος παῖς Διὸς ἱρέα ὃν
> αὐτὸς ἄγεν πάτρην ἐς ἀοίδιμον Εἰραφιώτης,
> ἐξόπιθεν δὲ θεῷ δωσιβίῳ πρόεσαν.
> 9 τοῖσι δ᾽ Ἀθηναίη πολιήοχος ἀντεβόλησε
> ἐρχομένοις Ῥειτώ, Χαλκιδικῷ ποταμῷ
> Θρειῶζ, ἔνθ᾽ ἁλίῳ συμβάλλετον οἶδμα ῥόος τε,
> 12 λαὸν ἄγουσα ἔτας πάντας ὁμηγερέας,
> ἱρῆας μὲν πρῶτα θεῶν κομόωντας ἐθείραις
> κόσμῳ τῷ σφετέρῳ, πάντας ἀριπρεπέας,
> 15 ἱρείας δὲ μεταῦθι σαόφρονα Κύπριν ἐχούσας,
> τῆς δ᾽ ἔπι κυδαλίμους παῖδας ἀοιδοπόλους
> Ζηνὶ θεηκολέοντας Ὀλυμπίωϊ μασικύδρους,
> 18 τοῖσι δ᾽ ἔπ᾽ ἠϊθέους ἵστορας ἠνορέης,
> παῖδας Ἀθηναίων χαλκῷ γανάοντας ἐφήβους,
> τοὺς αὐτός, λήθην πατρὸς ἀκειόμενος

21 Αἰγείδεω, λώβης δ(ν)οφοείμονος ἔσχεθε κοῦρο[υς]
   ἀργυφέαις χλαίναις οἴκοθεν ἀμφιέσας,
   δωρηθεὶς γ᾽ ἐνετῆσι κατωμαδὸν ἠλέκτροιο.
24 τῶν δ᾽ ὄπιθεν βουλὴ κεκριμένη Κεκρόπων
   ἔξαιτος προτέρω κίον ἀθρόοι, ἡ μὲν ἀρείω[ν],
   ἡ δ᾽ ἑτέρη μείων ἕσπετο τῇ κατόπιν.
27 πάντες δ᾽ ἐστολάδαντο νεόπλυτα φάρ[εα λευκά]·
   τῶν δ᾽ ἀνχοῦ προβάδην ἔστιχ[εν ἄλλος ὄχλος]
   ἐνδήμων ξείνων τε καὶ αι[- - - - -]
30 οὐδέ τις οἰκοφύλαξ λείπ[ετ᾽ ἐνὶ μεγάροις]
   οὐ παῖς, οὐ κούρη λευ[κώλενος, ἀλλ᾽ ἀγέροντο]
   δέγμενοι Ἡρώδην [- - - - - -]
33 ὡς δ᾽ ὅτε παῖδα γε[- - - - - - -]
   ἀμφιπέσῃ μή[τηρ- - - - - - - -]
   τηλόθεν ἐ[ξ ἀπίης γαίης - - - - - - -]
36 χαιροσύ[νῃ - - - - - - - - -]
   πλήν[- - - - - - - - -]
   ὦ[ρ]σ[ε;- - - - - - - -]

(O Happy Marathon, now people care about you much
more than before, as you behold the illustrious Alkaides, who
returned from Abia Sauromata at the ends of the earth, where
he followed the commander, the polemarch king of the Ausoni-
ans. And the ivy-wreathed son of Zeus, Eiraphiotes, himself led
his priest to the famous fatherland. The two life-giving goddesses came behind. Athena the patron met them, as they were
proceeding to the Rheitoi, to the two Chalcidian rivers in
Thria, where the swollen sea unites with the flow. She led the
assembled people; first the long-haired priests of the gods in
official order, all resplendent, then the priestesses with the pru-
dent Cypris (Aphrodite) in their midst; the renowned boy sing-
ers followed chanting hymns to Olympian Zeus. Behind them

came the new recruits, the valiant youths, sons of the Athenians, shimmering in bronze, the ephebes, which he, curing the forgetfulness of the father by Theseus, relieved the youths of the dark reproach and at his own (expense) clad them in white cloaks, presenting even fibulae of electrum for the shoulder. Behind came the elected boule of the Kekropians, the exceptional, further on, gathered together, walked first the noblest; the inferiors followed them behind. All wore freshly laundered white himations; near them proceeded the other folk, locals and foreigners and [slaves]; no one remained behind as guardian of the houses, neither boy nor tender girl, but they gathered to welcome Herodes [- - - - -] as when the son [- - - - - - - - - -] the mother embraces [- - - - - - - - - - - -] from a distant land [- - - - - - - - - - -]).

We learn from the inscription that all the Athenians took part in the procession. It was headed by the statue of Athena, followed by the long-haired priests in sacerdotal vestments, the statue of Aphrodite and the priestesses of Athena, a choir of boys singing hymns to Olympian Zeus, the newly recruited soldiers dressed in white cloaks, the boule of the Areopagos, the boule of the five hundred, and last the other residents of the city, Athenians, metics and slaves.

Herodes had also formed a procession. At its head was the statue of Dionysos, who bore the epithet *Eiraphiotes*, followed by the statue of Demeter and Kore. The meeting took place at Rheitoi, nowadays known as Lake Koumoundourou.

The two eroded marble heads (**11**, **12**) belong to busts of Herodes Atticus[183] and his pupil Polydeukion, and were found in 1955 near the tumulus at Marathon. Herodes is known to have set up herms with busts of himself or his pupils all over the

101-102

Fig. 101. Marble head of Herodes Atticus, no. 11, from the area of the Tumulus.

171

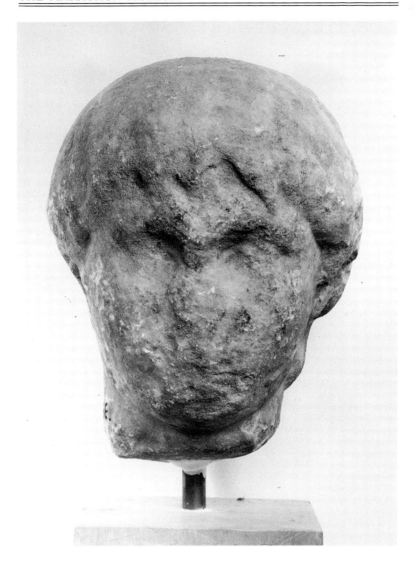

Fig. 102. Marble head of Polydeukion, no. 12, from the area of the Tumulus.

Marathon plain, near fountains, at crossroads and in sanctuaries.

The female head **16** represents Faustina the younger (AD **103** 125/30-175), wife of the Roman emperor Marcus Aurelius. Found some distance from Marathon, it probably came from some sanctuary for which it had been commissioned by Herodes Atticus.[184]

Head **101**, of an unknown man, dates from the third cen- **104** tury AD. Discovered at Marathon, it was inserted in a larger than life size statue.

Sculpture **25** is the left half of an enthroned figure, probably male. It may have embellished a wealthy house or been a votive offering in a sanctuary during the Roman period.

Impressive is the larger than life size statue **1**, 2.40 m high, in Egyptian style (2nd century AD), found in 1968 in the sanctuary of the Egyptian gods at Brexiza.[185]

A similar one was found at the same site in the nineteenth century and is now in the National Archaeological Museum, Athens. These statues stood left and right of the entrance to the sanctuary and portray the handsome favourite of the emperor Hadrian, Antinoos.

Statue **2**, also in the Egyptian style and contemporary with **1**, comes[186] from the same place. Only the lower part is preserved. The young woman represented was perhaps a member of the imperial court.

Exhibited on a special base is a beehive, used by the ancient Greeks as a child's coffin in the first century BC or the first century AD. The use of beehives as children's coffins was a common practice in antiquity.[187]

The funerary stele **108** shows a couple in frontal pose, copying the familiar statue types. The work is dated to the second **105** century AD, to the time of Herodes Atticus.

Fig. 103. Head of the empress Faustina the younger, no. 16, from the area of the Tumulus.

Fig. 104. Head from a marble statue of an unknown man, no. 101.

175

Fig. 105. Funerary stele no. 108, of two brothers, Alexander and Lenais.

Carved[188] on the architrave are the names of the figures:

'Αλέξανδρος 'Αντιγό-   Λnvαῖς 'Αντιγόνου ἐξ Αἰ-
νου Αἰϑαλίδης, ὁ καὶ 'Αντᾶς   ϑαλιδῶν

(Alexander, son of Antigonos of the deme of Aithalidai, named also Antas.

Lenais, daughter of Antigonos of the deme of Aithalidai).

Funerary stele **13** from Marathon presents personal traits **106** and is dated to the second century BC. Two men are depicted, the left one bearded and the right one clean-shaven and younger. Both hold a pruning tool in their right hand, while in his left the younger man also holds a vine which spreads out, laden with grapes, over the field of the relief. Between the two men is a calf. The sturdy bodies, the rustic attire and the distinctive elements —calf, vine, pruner— indicate that both men were farmers. According to the inscription[189] on the architrave, the man on the left was called *Ζωσᾶς* (Zosas), while the one of the right was *Νόστιμος Μειλήσιος* (Nostimos a Milesian).

Sculpture **122**, of Pentelic marble, shows a larger than life **107** size, half-naked man reclining on a luxurious couch. In his right hand he held a circular object. Marinatos[190] suggested that the recumbent male perhaps represented a river god (Charadros of Marathon?), a hero or even a mere mortal.

The bed, mattress and pillow are rendered in realistic manner. The bed is ornamented with rosettes in front, and with alternating lozenges and rectangles on the inside of the other three sides. The mattress bears relief bands, corresponding to the coloured stripes of the material.

The sculpture was found in what is considered to be the Pythion at Oinoe, which was most probably constructed by Herodes Atticus. The couch with the reclining male is dated to the same period as the Pythion.

Fig. 106. Funerary stele no. 13, of Zosas and Nostimos.

Fig. 107. Male reclining on a couch, no. 122, from the Pythion at Oinoe.

Also associated with Marathon is the famous bronze statue known as the ephebe of Marathon (EAM 15118). Found by fishermen in June 1925, on the seabed of the gulf of Marathon, it actually portrays Hermes. There is no evidence to associate this work with Marathon and the speculation, one of many, that it was perhaps used as a lampstand in Herodes' villa interprets neither its original provenance nor its initial purpose.

COURTYARD

At the centre of the Museum is a courtyard in which several antiquities are displayed; some have been described, such as the lintel of the temple of the Egyptian gods at Brexiza, with the relief solar disc surrounded by the snake (p. 79), the ashlar block (**129**) with the name 'Αλκία (p. 94) and the topmost section —keystone and two voussoirs— of the stone arch (p. 102) of the gateway to Herodes' estate at Mandra tes Grias, inscribed on both faces Ὁμονοίας ἀθανάτου πύλη (Gateway of Immortal Harmony). As we have seen, on the inside of the gateway, in front of the two jambs, Herodes had set up two statues of enthroned figures (Herodes and Regilla). The remains of these works (**158, 159**) are exhibited here, even though badly eroded by one thousand eight hundred years and more of exposure to the elements.

Of the *ex-votos* of Herodes, of which we have spoken at length, exhibited in the courtyard are sections of two herms; one (**213**) bears an imprecation of Herodes and the other (**214**) an inscription concerning his Ethiopian pupil Memnon (Μέμνων τοπάδειν Ἀρτ[έμιδος] φ[ίλος] (Memnon, little topaz, beloved of Artemis).

The two Ionic column capitals with the typical rough working of the surface of the marble and the dessicated aspect that gives these members a purely decorative character, date from the Roman period. Comparison with the Ionic column capital of the trophy (p. 135-136, figs 74-75) reveals that their crafstmen no longer understood the tectonic function of these members, which lack the soul and the internal dynamism of their counterparts of earlier times.

Two funerary monuments of the fourth century BC. The body of a lion (**75**) found at the side of the road leading from Marathon to Kato Souli, where the pumping station stands today and where some tomb stood in antiquity. The large eroded grave stele of the same period (**130**) was found on Penteli. It shows a seated female left, perhaps the deceased, greeting a standing female right. Between the two women, in the background of the stele, a standing slave girl holds a pyxis, that is the jewellery box of her dead mistress. The relief is not the work of an accomplished sculptor but of some humble marble carver in the ancient quarries in the Dionysos area. This is evident from the modelling of the figures, the proportions of the stele and the inordinately large pediment.

The remaining funerary stelae are later. The section of a stele (**36**) with the inscription Σέλευκος Ξενοχά[ρους]/Φλυεύς (Seleukos, son of Xenochares of Phlya) dates to the first century BC, and the section of what is probably a pedestal, of grey stone (**38**), with the name Εὐκλῆς Ἡρώδου Μαραθών[ιος] (Eukles, son of Herodes of Marathon), to the first century AD. The intact stele **212** is typical of the turn of the second to the third century AD. It shows a youth, Paramonos, in frontal **108** pose, almost nude, upon a pedestal. Left is his mother who embraces him protectively. Right is his father, Euodos, also standing, his right arm concealed under his himation. Of interest is the epigram incised on the architrave, above the heads of the figures, excerpts from which are quoted: Παράμονος Εὐόδου Πειρεύς, ἔφηβος ᾿Αθηναῖος, πλειστάκις εὐφρανθεὶς ὀλίγοις/ἔ- τεσιν μετὰ πολλῶν, ὧδε κάτω κεῖμαι βαθεῖ βεβλημένος ὕπνῳ (I, Paromonos, son of Euodos, from Piraeus, Athenian ephebe, having been delighted many times in the space of a few years, together with several others, am here below [in the earth] smitten by a deep sleep). The delights Paramonos had sampled were the joys of life with other children and with his companions as an ephebe, in exercise, instruction, marches and processions. The poetic concept of the age, of the transcendence after death to a higher sphere, to the ranks of the heroes, is apparent in the phrase with which the epigram concludes: σὺν Κάστορι καὶ Πολυδεύκῃ ἄστρων χῶρον ἔχων, Θησεὺς εἰμὶ νέος (I am a star, together with Castor and Pollux, I am the new Theseus). The paralleling of Theseus with the Dioscuri is not fortuitous; he was the paramount hero of Athens and was linked with Castor and Pollux through their sister, Helen.

Fig. 108. Funerary stele of Paramonos, from Piraeus.

Abbreviations

The following abbreviations are used in the notes:

AAA	Ἀρχαιολογικὰ Ἀνάλεκτα ἐξ Ἀθνῶν
ΑΔ	Ἀρχαιολογικὸν Δελτίον
AJA	American Journal of Archaeology
AJPh	American Journal of Philology
AM	Athenische Mitteilungen
BSA	Annual of the British School at Athens
CAH	Cambridge Ancient History
CIG	Corpus Inscriptionum Graecarum
ClPh	Classical Philology
CVA	Corpus Vasorum Antiquorum, Grèce 1
Ἔργον	Τὸ Ἔργον τῆς ἐν Ἀθήναις Ἀρχαιολογικῆς Ἑταιρείας
IG	Inscriptiones Graecae
JHS	Journal of Hellenic Studies
ΠΑΑ	Πρακτικὰ τῆς Ἀκαδημίας Ἀθηνῶν
ΠΑΕ	Πρακτικὰ τῆς ἐν Ἀθήναις Ἀρχαιολογικῆς Ἑταιρείας
RA	Revue Archéologique
SEG	Supplementum Epigraphicum Graecum
SGHI	A Selection of Greek Historical Inscriptions
ZPE	Zeitschrift für Papyrologie und Epigraphik

Notes

1. Plut., *Theseus* 32, 4.
2. I 15, 3 and I 32, 4.
3. Athen., *Deipn.* II 56 c.
4. C. Blümel, *Die archaisch griechischen Skulpturen der Staatlichen Museen zu Berlin* 20 no. 12 figs 29-33.
5. *Scholia Plat. Men.* 240 c.
6. Lines 245-246.
7. Pind., *Olymp.* 13, 110 (157).
8. Non., *Dionys.* 13, 184.
9. Herod. VI 102.
10. Ibidem 106-107.
11. Ibidem 107.
12. Ibidem 107.
13. Ibidem I 62.
14. *Qrations* 1411a. See also Corn. Nep., *Miltiades* 5.
15. VI 109.
16. Herod., VI 110.
17. Ibidem 111-112.
18. Ibidem 113.
19. N. Hammond, *Studies in Greek History* 196.
20. VI 112.
21. Ibidem 113.
22. Ibidem 117.
23. I 32, 5.
24. *Theseus* 35, 2.
25. Aelian, *On animals* VI 38.
26. VI 114.
27. N. Hammond, *JHS* 88, 1968, 39 ff. *CAH²* IV 511.
28. I 32, 3.
29. *Miltiades* 5.

30. N. Hammond, *CAH*² IV 516. Largely unknown is the exhaustive description and analysis of the evidence on the battle by General Leonidas Lapathiotis, in *Νέα 'Εστία* 20, 1936, 900-905, 1021-1027, 1068-1072, 1146-1152.
31. VI 115.
32. VI 124. See also A. Trevor Hodge and Luis A. Losada, The time of the Shield Signal at Marathon, *AJA* 73, 1969, 31-36. Earlier publications on the same subject, R.K. Baillie Reynolds, *JHS* 49, 1929, 100-105, R.B. Henderson, *JHS* 52, 1932, 302-303.
33. Marcell., *Life of Thucydides* 54.
34. *Acharnes* 179-181.
35. *Σορὸς* means coffin, vase for the bones of the dead, grave or even the corpse. It is sometimes written *Σωρὸς* which today also means a mound of earth.
36. II 34, 5-6.
37. I 32, 3.
38. *IG* II² 1006, 69 ff.
39. Ibidem 1035, 33; *Hesperia* 44, 1975, 213.
40. I 32, 3.
41. VII 15, 7. The issues of the separate burial of the dead slaves and the political rights of the survivors are examined by J.A. Notopoulos, *AJPh* 62, 1941, 353-354. Concerning the according of honours to those slaves who fell for the freedom of Athens, A. Raubitschek (*Hesperia* 14, 1945, 368) draws attention too to the passage in Pausanias I 29, 7: *'ἦν δὲ ἄρα καὶ δήμου δίκαιον βούλευμα, εἰ δὴ καὶ 'Αθηναῖοι μετέδοσαν δούλοις δημοσίᾳ ταφῆναι καὶ τὰ ὀνόματα ἐγγραφῆναι στήλῃ'* (It was surely a just decree of the people when the Athenians actually allowed slaves a public funeral, and to have their names inscribed on a slab).
42. I 32, 4.
43. *Topographie d'Athènes* (trans. Ph. Roque, Malta 1849) 147; *Travels in Northern Greece* II 431, *Die Demen von Attika* 84. The earth of the tumulus seen by Leake had been extracted by the ancient Greeks from an area with prehistoric remains. Leake also notes the information that he and others had found bronze arrow heads on the site of the tumulus. On the provenance of arrow heads from the battlefield see W. Kendrick Pritchett, *Marathon* 159-160 and Elisabeth Erdmann, *AA* 1973, 30-58. It was fashionable for nineteenth-century travellers to collect arrow

heads, perhaps as a result of what Leake had written. For this reason the Minister of Education, Iakovos Rizos Neroulos, issued the following document (12 May 1836) to the Provincial Directorate of Attica (GSA, Antiquities, General, ϑ 123 fol. 2: 'Being informed that foreign travellers passing via Marathon are frequently excavating, with the help of the locals, in the very tumulus of those Athenians who fell in the battle (the so-called mound), in order to find arrow heads, and wishing this most ancient monument of Greek glory to remain untouched and untroubled, we ask you to issue as quickly as possible the necessary orders to the municipal authority of Marathon, so that it is not allowed for anyone on any pretext to excavate the afore-mentioned tumulus or the other monuments on the field of battle'.

44. *Zeitschrift für Ethnologie*, Berlin 1884, 85 ff. An excavation by Fauvel on 20 October 1788 is also attested. *RA* 30, 1897, 55 (Ph.E. Legrand).

45. Δύο λέξεις περὶ τοῦ πῶς γράφονται τὰ τῶν ἀνασκαφῶν (Athens 1890).

46. *AΔ* 1890, 65-71; 123-132, pl. Δ. Βαλέριος Στάης, *AM* 18, 1893, 46-63, pls II-V.

47. *Topographische, archäologische und militärische Betrachtungen auf dem Schlachtfelde von Marathon* (Berlin 1886) 10. On the number of dead Persians see Harry C. Avery, *Historia* 22, 1973, 756 and William F. Wyatt, Jr., *Historia* 25, 1976, 483-484.

48. VI 117.

49. I 32, 5.

50. Ποικίλη Ἱστορία II 25.

51. *Anabasis* 3, 2, 11 ff. and Aristoph., *Knights* 660 and the ancient commentary according to which 'Καλλίμαχος ὁ πολέμαρχος λέγεται εὔξα-σθαι τῇ Ἀρτέμιδι τοσαύτας βοῦς, ὅσους ἂν φονεύσῃ βαρβάρους ἐν Μαραθῶνι· ἐπειδὴ δὲ πολλοὶ ἐφονεύθησαν μὴ δυνάμενος τοσαύτας βοῦς θῦσαι ἔθυσε χιμαίρας' (It is said that Callimachus the polemarch pledged to Artemis as many cows as Persians he slew at Marathon; but because many were killed, unable to sacrifice so many cows he sacrificed she-goats). With considerable licence the scholiast overlooks the fact that Callimachus had been slain in the battle and could not possibly have made the sacrifice. The story is mentioned in Plutarch's essay, Περὶ τῆς Ἡροδότου κακοηθείας 862 b-c.

52. Ch. Seltman, *Greek Coins* 92-93 pl. XII, 16, 17.

53. Xenoph., *Cyropaedia* II 3, 2.

54. *Aristides* 5, 5.
55. I 32, 4. Published by E. Vanderpool, *Hesperia* 35, 1966, 93-106.
56. *Knights* 1334; *Wasps* 711; *Lysistrate* 285.
57. Diels-Kranz, *Die Fragmente der Vorsokratiker* II 377. In earlier times the ancient Greeks avoided founding permanent victory trophies so as not to perpetuate animosity between the adversaries. Diod. Sicul. 13, 24, 5-6: 'τίνος γὰρ χάριν οἱ πρόγονοι πάντων τῶν Ἑλλήνων ἐν ταῖς κατὰ πόλεμον νίκαις κατέδειξαν οὐ διὰ λίθων, διὰ δὲ τῶν τυχόντων ξύλων ἱστάναι τὰ τρόπαια; ἆρ' οὐχ ὅπως ὀλίγον χρόνον διαμένοντα ταχέως ἀφανίζηται τὰ τῆς ἔχθρας ὑπομνήματα;' (For what reason did the ancestors of all the Greeks ordain that the trophies set up in celebrating victories in war should be made, not of stone, but of any wood at hand? Was it not in order that the memorials of the enmity, lasting as they would for a brief time, should quickly disappear?). William C. West III, *ClPh* 64, 1969, 6-19 explains that the monument that the ancient Greeks characterized as the trophy of the battle of Marathon was in form and concept an *ex-voto*.
58. 240 d.
59. *Εἰς Καλλίμαχον* 61. There is a summary corresponding description in Plutarch, *Συναγωγὴ ἱστοριῶν παραλλήλων ἑλληνικῶν καὶ ρωμαϊκῶν* (*Parallela Graeca et Romana*) 305 C: 'Καλλίμαχος δὲ πολλοῖς περιπεπαρμένος δόρασι καὶ νεκρὸς ἑστάθη' (Callimachus stood upright though pierced with many spears and already dead).
60. *Πότερον Ἀθναῖοι κατὰ πόλεμον ἢ κατὰ σοφίαν ἐνδοξότεροι* (Bellone an pace clariores fuerint Athenienses) 347 C.
61. *Ὑπὲρ τοῦ ἐν τῇ προσαγορεύσει πταίσματος* (A slip of the tongue in greeting) 3.
62. *JHS* 88, 1968, 39.
63. Herod. VI 105.
64. Ibidem 120.
65. Meiggs-Lewis, *SGHI* 19; *IG* I³ 1463.
66. X 10, 1-2.
67. I 28, 2.
68. I 15, 3.
69. IX 4.
70. I 32, 4.
71. VI 105.

72. D.L. Page, *Further Greek Epigrams* 194-195.
73. Ibidem 225-231.
74. *Κατὰ Λεωκράτους* 109. '*Τοιγαροῦν ἐπὶ τοῖς ἠρίοις μαρτύρια ἔστιν ἰδεῖν τῆς ἀρετῆς αὐτῶν ἀναγεγραμμένα ἀληθῆ πρὸς ἅπαντας τοὺς "Ελληνας*' (And so over there graves a testimony to their coverage can be seen faithfully engraved for every Greek to read).
75. In s.v. '*Ποικίλη· στοὰ ἐν 'Αθήναις ἔνθα ἐγράφησαν οἱ ἐν Μαραθῶνι πολεμήσαντες, εἰς οὕς ἐστιν ἐπίγραμμα τόδε*' (Poikile, portico in Athens where were depicted those who fought at Marathon, for whom there is the following epigram).
76. E. Vanderpool, *ΑΔ* 24, 1969 A, 1-2; P. Amandry, *BCH* 95, 1971, 602 ff.; Μαρ. Σ. Μπρούσκαρη, *Τὸ Μουσεῖο Παύλου καὶ 'Αλεξάνδρας Κανελλοπούλου* 69; *IG* I³ 523.
77. XI 33, 3.
78. *IG* II² 1006 cols 26-27.
79. *Πότερον 'Αθηναῖοι κατὰ πόλεμον ἢ κατὰ σοφίαν ἐνδοξότεροι* 349 E. Noteworthy is the use of the name of Marathon during the French Revolution. Indeed, on 25 brumaire of year II (1793), it was officially requested that the name of the town of Saint-Maximin be changed to Marathon. According to the application of the People's Committee of Saint-Maximin: 'Marathon is the name we have chosen: that sacred name reminds us of the Athenian plain that became the grave of one hundred thousand spear-bearers; but it brings to mind with greater clarity the Friend of the People. Marat was a victim of the federalists and conspirators. God grant that the name we have chosen will help keep eternal his virtues and his patriotism' (Claude Mossé, *L'Antiquité dans la Revolution française* (1989) 133-134).
80. N. Hammond, *JHS* 88, 1968, 40. Opinion is divided concerning the day and the month of the battle. See A.R. Burn, *Persia and the Greeks* 256.
81. *Declamatio* XII, *Timonis oratio* 38.
82. Dion. Halic. 7, 3, 1; *SEG* 10, 352.
83. Herod. VI 104.
84. *CIG* 6088; Kaibel, *Epigr. Gr.* 1087; *SEG* 13, 479; G. Pfohl, *Griechische Inschriften* 87.
85. M. Bieber, *AJA* 58, 1954, 282 ff.
86. XLVI 161, 13.
87. Paus. I 18, 3.

88. *Bull. Epigr.* 1962, 137; L. Robert, *ΣΤΗΛΗ, τόμος εἰς μνήμην N. Κοντολέοντος* 15 note 46.

89. VIII 52, 1.

90. E. Kunze, *Gnomon* 1954, 192; G. Pfohl, *Griechische Inschriften* no. 51. Νικ. Παπαχατζῆ, *Παυσανίου Ἑλλάδος περιήγησις* III 365; *IG* I³ 1472.

91. Plut., *Aristides* 5, 5. *IG* I³ 1467.

92. I 32, 4.

93. *Die Demen von Attika* (trans. Westermann) 85.

94. The epigram was attributed to Aeschylus by the ancient Greeks, but this is disputed by modern research; see D.L. Page, *Further Greek Epigrams* 131-132.

95. I 14, 5.

96. *Deipn.* XIV 627 c-d.

97. Herod. VI 114.

98. *IG* I² 609; B.B. Shefton, *BSA* 45, 1950, 140-164, pls 10-11; for the full bibliography and the various discrepancies in the completion of the epigram see *IG* I³ 784. The text here is based on Raubitschek's completion, first published by Shefton op. cit. See also *SEG* 38, 17.

99. Herod. VI 108.

100. *IG* I³ 2-3 see also p. 935. Main bibliography: E. Vanderpool, *Hesperia* II, 1942, 329-337; *SEG* 10, 2; 34, 1; 36, 1; Pritchett, *ClPh* 49, 1954, 42; E. Vanderpool, *AJA* 70, 1966, 322-323 and *Studies presented to Sterling Dow* 295-296. D. Whitehead, *The Demes of Attica* (1986) 36-37. For the text and translation of the inscription see the chapter describing the exhibit in the museum pp. 137-138.

101. Σπ. Μαρινάτος, *ΠΑΕ* 1972, 6; Στ. Ν. Κουμανούδης, *AAA* 11, 1978, 237-242. The second publication gives the interpretation offered here. The completion by W. Peek, Attische Versinschriften, *ASAW* 69, 2, 1980, 34-35 no. 34 does not seem probable. New edition with bibliography *IG* I³ 1015 bis.

102. I 32, 4.

103. IX 88 ff.

104. VIII 79.

105. *Θεῶν ἐκκλησία* 7.

106. 8, 377.

107. Γ. Σωτηριάδης, *ΠΑΕ* 1935, 156-158.

108. J.R. McCredie, *Hesperia*, Suppl. XI (1966) 35.

109. I 32, 5.
110. I 32, 6.
111. *Lysistrata* 1032.
112. In the epigram attributed to him about the battle of Marathon.
113. I 14, 5.
114. I 32, 7.
115. Σπ. Μαρινάτος, *AAA* 3, 1970, 63-67, 153-154, 349. *ΠΑΕ* 1970, 5-9. Εὐθ. Μαστροκώστας, *AAA* 3, 1970, 14-21.
116. Σπ. Μαρινάτος, *AAA* 3, 1970, 67, 154-155, 349-350, 364. *Ἔργον* 1970, 5-8; 1971, 5-7; 1972, 5. *ΠΑΕ* 1971, 5-6; 1972, 5.
117. *AAA* 3, 1970, 68, 155-156, 351-366. *ΠΑΕ* 1970, 9-18, 20-28; 1972, 5.
118. *ΠΑΕ* 1933, 35-38; 1934, 35-38; *ΠΑΑ* 9, 1934, 261-279.
119. *Ἔργον* 1958, 23-27.
120. XXIII 237-261. ʹαὐτοῦ λαὸν ἔρυκε καὶ ἵζανεν εὐρὺν ἀγῶνα, / νηῶν δʹ ἔκφερʹ ἄεθλα λέβητάς τε τρίποδάς τε / ἵππους θʹ ἡμιόνους τε βοῶν τʹ ἴφθιμα κάρηνα, / ἠδὲ γυναῖκας ἐϋζώνους πολιόν τε σίδηρον.ʹ (But Achilles stayed the folk even where they were, and made them sit in a wide gathering; and from his ships brought forth prizes; cauldrons and tripods and horses and mules and strong oxen and fair-girdled women and grey iron).
121. *ΠΑΕ* 1958, 15-17.
122. *ΠΑΕ* 1970, 18.
123. Ibidem 20-28.
124. D. Callipolitis-Feytmans, *AAA* 4, 1971, 99-101.
125. *IG* I³ 1362.
126. I 32, 3.
127. *ΠΑΕ* 1933, 31-35, 41-42; 1934, 30-35; 1935, 92-106; *ΠΑΑ* 9, 1934, 14-16.
128. Γ. Σωτηριάδης, *ΠΑΕ* 1933, 42, 44; 1935, 90.
129. *AJA* 70, 1966, 322. According to the literary and epigraphic tradition Athena was worshipped at Marathon with the eponym *Hellotis*. Mentioned in the calendar of the sacrifices of the Tetrapolis are the offerings made to her and that her sanctuary was called *Hellotion*. For the relevant testimonies see S. Solders, *Die ausserstädtischen Kulte und die Einigung Attikas* (1931) 15, IV. Moreover, Athena was depicted in the large wall-painting of the battle of Marathon, in the Poikile Stoa at Athens, along with Theseus and Heracles.

130. Excerpt from the biography of Fauvel, *RA* 30, 1897, 56 (Ph.-E. Legrand).

131. Ἡμερολόγιον τῆς Μεγάλης Ἑλλάδος (1933) 536.

132. Ἀ. Βαβρίτσας, *AAA* 1, 1968, 230-234. J. Travlos, *Bildlexikon zur Topographie des antiken Attika* 218-219.

133. *Lives of the Sophists* 554.

134. Ibidem 552-553.

135. Ξένη Ἀραπογιάννη, *AE* 1993, 133-186.

136. IV.

137. VI 105.

138. I 32, 6.

139. Ἔργον 1958, 15-22. Β.Χ. Πετράκος, *Μέντωρ* 25, 1993, 67-70.

140. Β.Χ. Πετράκος, *Φίλια Ἔπη εἰς Γεώργιον Ε. Μυλωνᾶν*, Β´, 305-306; *SEG* 36, 267.

141. *ΠΑΕ* 1972, 6-7; J. Travlos, *Bildlexikon Attika* 217-218, figs 294-301.

142. Βιβλιοθήκη II 5, 7.

143. VII 80.

144. The bibliography on Herodes Atticus, his life and work, is extensive and can be summarized in two basic works on the sophist: P. Graindor, *Hérode Atticus et sa famille* (Le Caire 1930); W. Ameling, *Herodes Atticus*, I. *Biographie*, II. *Inschriftenkatalog* (G. Olms 1983).

145. Γ. Σωτηριάδης, *ΠΑΕ* 1935, 149-150; J.R. MacCredie, *Hesperia*, Suppl. XI (1966) 35-37; A. Mallwitz, *AM* 79, 1964, 157-164; E. Vanderpool, *Hesperia* 39, 1970, 43-45.

146. *IG* II² 5189.

147. Γ. Σωτηριάδης, *ΠΑΕ* 1933, 32; E. Vanderpool, *Hesperia* 39, 1970, 43-45, pl. 4.

148. D.J. Geagan, *AM* 79, 1964, 149-156.

149. *Lives of the Sophists* 558-559.

150. *IG* II² 4774.

151. Ibidem 3970.

152. Ibidem 3973.

153. Ibidem 3977.

154. Ibidem 13195.

155. *The Life of Apollonius of Tyana* III 11.

156. *IG* II² 13196 and *SEG* 35, 210.

157. R. Merkelbach, *ZPE* 48, 1982, 218.

158. Β.Χ. Πετράκος, *ΑΔ* 17, 1961/62, Β, 29-30, pls 32, 34.

159. *Lives of the Sophists* 559.

160. Jennifer Tobin, *AJA* 95, 1991, 336.

161. P. Graindor, *Hérode Atticus* 111.

162. *Lives of the Sophists* 559.

163. Ibidem 562.

164. Ibidem 571.

165. First published by E. Vanderpool, *Hesperia* 35, 1966, 93-106, pls 31-35. See idem, *Hesperia* 36, 1967, 108-110, pl. 31.

166. *Themistocles* 3, 4.

167. Γ. Σωτηριάδης, *ΠΑΕ* 1932, 42; Γ. Δ. ᾿Ανδρουτσόπουλος, *Πολέμων* 3, 1947/48, 131.

168. See also the chapter on topography p. 50 (Heracleion).

169. See note 100.

170. The pottery from the excavation of the tumulus was published by Σέμνη Καρούζου, *CVA* Athènes, Musée National I pp. 6-8, pls 10-14. See also Chr. W. Clairmont, *Patrios Nomos* I 98-101. Detailed references are given at the end of the book (p. 195).

171. *ΑΔ* 1890, 131. Herod. VI 114.

172. See chapter on the excavation of the tumulus, pp. 22-24.

173. ᾿Αθ. Καλογεροπούλου, *ΑΔ* 29, 1974, Α, 194-225 ff., figs 1-4, pls 125-132.

174. ῎Αγγ. Λιάγκουρας, *ΑΔ* 29, 1974, Β1, 66, pl. 67a.

175. ᾿Αθ. Καλογεροπούλου, *Πρακτικά Γ´ ᾿Επιστημονικῆς Συνάντησης ΝΑ. ᾿Αττικῆς, Καλύβια 1988*, 107-115, figs. 1-4.

176. Κωστῆς Δαβάρας, *ΑΔ* 20, 1965, Β1, 123.

177. *IG* II² 7296.

178. Εὐθ. Μαστροκώστας, *ΑΑΑ* 3, 1970, 19; G. Daux, *BCH* 94, 1970, 607; J.P. Michaud, ibidem 919; *SEG* 32, 306.

179. Α.Κ. Βαβρίτσας, *ΑΑΑ* 3, 1968, 230, fig. 5.

180. ῎Αγγ. Λιάγκουρας, *ΑΔ* 29, 1973/74, Β, 64-67, pl. 67; *SEG* 29, 278.

181. Ibidem.

182. *IG* II² 3606.

183. Herodes: ᾿Αλ. Σταυρίδη, *ΑΑΑ* 11, 1978, 220 note 4 (identified by G. Despinis). Polydeukion: ᾿Αλ. Σταυρίδη, *ΑΑΑ* 10, 1977, 146, fig. 23.

184. ᾿Αλ. Σταυρίδη, *ΑΑΑ* 11, 1978, 220 note 4.

185. ᾿Α. Βαβρίτσας, *ΑΑΑ* 1, 1968, 230-234, figs 1-4. The two male statues

were identified as Antinoos by 'Αλ. Σταυρίδη, 'Αρχαιογνωσία 1, 1980, 347-348, pls 25-26. The statue in the National Museum (Egyptian Collection 1), Ph. Le Bas, *Voyage archéologique, Monuments figurés* III (Paris 1847-68) pl. 31; L. v. Sybel, *Katalog der Skulpturen zu Athen* (1881) 7-8 no. 39; A. Milchhöfer, *AM* 12, 1887, 310 no. 316.

186. 'Α. Βαβρίτσας, *AAA* 1, 1968, 230-234.

187. "Αγγ. Λιάγκουρας, *ΑΔ* 29, 1974, B1, pl. 67γ.

188. *SEG* 25, 239.

189. *IG* II^2 9631.

190. *ΠΑΕ* 1972, 7, pl. 3γ.

Publications of the pottery and the minor arts in the Marathon Museum

CASE 1. 361: Chr. Zervos, *Naissance de la Civilisation en Grèce* (France 1963) II 550, pls 832-33. **1357:** Ι. Παπαδημητρίου, *Έργον* 1958, 19, fig. 18. Zervos op. cit. 551, pl. 843.

CASE 2. 641: Παπαδημητρίου op. cit. 19, fig. 17; Zervos op. cit. 551, pl. 828.

Sherds with grooved decoration: Zervos op. cit. 550.

CASE 3. 673 and **1396:** Παπαδημητρίου op. cit. 20, fig. 19; Zervos op. cit. 550, pl. 841. **Beads in vase 673:** Παπαδημητρίου op. cit. 20, fig. 20. **1401:** Zervos op. cit. pl. 829.

CASE 4. 74: Σπ. Μαρινάτος, *ΠΑΕ* 1970, 9, pl. 34γ; *Έργον* 1971, 7, figs 3-4; *ΠΑΕ* 1971, 6, pl. 2. **58:** idem, *AAA* 3, 1970, 350, fig. 4. **39:** ibidem fig. 32.

CASE 6. 6: Σπ. Μαρινάτος, *ΠΑΕ* 1970, 13, pl. 14α. **7:** ibidem pl. 146. **3:** ibidem pl. 136. **1:** ibidem 11, pl. 11α. **458:** ibidem 16, pl. 21α-6; idem, *AAA* 3, 1970, 336, fig. 11. **20:** idem, *ΠΑΕ* 1970, 16, pl. 21γ; idem, *AAA* 3, 1970, 337, fig. 12. **26:** idem, *ΠΑΕ* 1970, 18, pl. 25α. **27:** ibidem pl. 25γ. **22:** ibidem pl. 256. **25:** ibidem pl. 25α. **23:** ibidem pl. 256.

CASE 7. 836: Γ. Σωτηριάδης, *ΠΑΕ* 1939, 34, fig. 5α. **842:** ibidem fig. 56. **846:** ibidem fig. 3v; J. Coldstream, *Greek Geometric Pottery* (London 1968) 13, 16. **79:** Σωτηριάδης op. cit. 31, fig. 1α; Coldstream op. cit. 16. **853:** Σωτηριάδης op. cit. 34, fig. 4; Coldstream op. cit. 16.

CASE 8. 107: R. Tölle, *Frühgriechische Reigentänze* (1964) 16 no. 23; Goldstream op. cit. 60, no. 44, pl. 11. **95:** Γ. Σωτηριάδης, *ΠΑΕ* 1934, 35, fig. 8. **82:** ibidem 35, fig. 7. **845:** ibidem 33, fig. 2; Coldstream op. cit. 13. **108:** Γ. Σωτηριάδης, *ΠΑΕ* 1934; fig. 9; Coldstream op. cit. 75, no. 8.

Child burials: Γ. Σωτηριάδης, *ΠΑΕ* 1934, 38. **1477:** Εὐθ. Μαστροκώστας, *AAA* 3, 1970, 17, fig. 3.

CASE 10. 737 (1011): B. Στάης, *AM* 18, 1893, 52, fig. 5; M. Collignon - L. Couve, *Catalogue des vases peints du Musée National d'Athènes* (Paris 1902) no. 947; C.H.E. Haspels, *Attic Black Figured Lekythoi*, Appendix X, no. 1 pl. 30, 3; *CVA* Grèce 1, pl. 11, no. 9. **738** (1012): Hespels op. cit. no. 10; *CVA* pl. 11, no. 3. **739** (1013): Haspels op. cit. no. 8; *CVA* pl. 11, no. 10. **740** (1014): ibidem pl. 11, no. 8; Haspels op. cit. no. 9. **741** (1015): ibidem no. 11; *CVA* pl. 11, no. 6. **745** (1019): B. Στάης, *AΔ* 6, 1890, pl. Δ, 7; G. Perrot - Ch. Chipier, *Histoire de l'art dans l'antiquité* (Paris 1903) VIII 87, no. 52; *CVA* pl. 10, no. 1. **746** (1020): ibidem, pl. 11, no. 2. **747** (1021): ibidem pl. 11, no. 4. **749** (1023): ibidem pl. 10, no. 6. **750** (1024): B. Στάης, *AM* 18, 1893, 51, fig. 2; Collignon - Couve op. cit. no. 946; *CVA* pl. 10, no. 5. **751** (1025): ibidem pl. 10, no. 10. **752** (1026): ibidem pl. 10, no. 3. **753** (1027): ibidem pl. 10, no. 2. **754** (1028): ibidem pl. 10, no. 13. **755** (1029): Haspels op. cit. no. 12; *CVA* pl. 11, no. 5. **756** (1030): ibidem pl. 11, no. 1. **757** (1031): ibidem pl. 11, no. 11. **758** (1033): ibidem pl. 10, no. 12. **759** (1034): ibidem pl. 10, no. 11. **760** (1035): ibidem pl. 10, no. 4. **762α** (1037): B. Στάης, *AM* 18, 1893, 61 ff., pl. V, 1; Collignon - Couve·op. cit. no. 767; *CVA* pl. 14, nos 1-2. **7626** (1038): B. Στάης, *AΔ* 6, 1890, 131, pl. Δ, 5; Perrot - Chipier op. cit. 87, fig. 53; E. Pfuhl, *Malerei und Zeichnung der Griechen* (München 1923) XI 28; *CVA* pl. 11 no. 7. **763** (1093): ibidem pl. 10, no. 15. **764α** (1040): B. Στάης, *AΔ* 7, 1891, 69, no. 4; idem, *AM* 18, 1893, 59 ff., pl. IV; Collignon - Couve op. cit. no. 836; *CVA* pl. 10, nos 7-8. **7646** (1041): ibidem pl. 13, no. 3. **766** (1043): B. Στάης, *AM* 18, 1893, 55 ff., pl. III; Collignon - Couve op. cit. no. 607; *CVA* pl. 12, nos 1-2. **847** (1042): B. Στάης, *AΔ* 6, 1890, pl. Δ, 9; *CVA* pl. 13, no. 4. **848** (1044): B. Στάης, *AM* 18, 1893, 63, pl. V, 2; *CVA* pl. 13, no. 5. **850** (1032): ibidem pl. 11, no. 13. **EAM 1036:** B. Στάης, *AΔ* 7, 1891, 69, no. 1; Hauvette, *Archives des Missions* II (1892) 334, pl. III; B. Στάης, *AM* 18, 1893, 57, pl. II; Collignon - Couve op. cit. no. 592; Pfuhl op. cit. 121, fig. 90; E. Pottier, *Musée National du Louvre. Catalogue des vases antiques de terre cuite* (Paris 1928) 649; S. Papaspiridi-Karusu, *AM* 62, 1937, 117, 119, 128, 134, no. 35, pls 61-62; P. Mingazzini, *ASAtene* 36-37, 1974-1975, 9-13.

'Marathon Painter' (lekythoi **737-741**): Haspels op. cit. 77, 87 ff. Appendix X figs 30, 31.

CASE 11. 154: Σπ. Μαρινάτος, *ΠΑΕ* 1970, 25, pl. 38ϐ. **155:** idem, *AAA* 3, 1970, fig. 27. **156:** idem, *AAA* 3, 1970, fig. 22; D. Callipolitis-Feytmans, *AAA* 4, 1971, 99-101, fig. 1. **157:** Σπ. Μαρινάτος, *ΠΑΕ* 1970, 25, pl. 38α; idem, *AAA* 3, 1970, fig. 21; D. Callipolitis-Feytmans, *AAA* 4, 1971, 99-101, fig. 2. **158, 159:** Σπ. Μαρινάτος, *ΠΑΕ* 1970, 25, pl. 38ϐ; idem, *AAA* 3, 1970, fig. 28. **160:** idem, *Έργον* 1970, 12-13; idem, *ΠΑΕ* 1970, 25, pl. 39ϐ; idem, *AAA* 3, 1970, 361, fig. 26. **161:** idem, *ΠΑΕ* 1970, 25, pl. 34α; idem, *AAA* 3, 1970, 361, fig. 24; Π.Γ. Θέμελης, *ΑΔ* 29, 1974, Α, 244. **162, 175:** Σπ. Μαρινάτος, *ΠΑΕ* 1970, 25, pl. 37ϐ; idem, *AAA* 3, 1970, fig. 29. **163:** idem, *ΠΑΕ* 1970, 25, pl. 34ϐ· idem, *AAA* 3, 1970, 361, εἰκ. 23. **164:** idem, *ΠΑΕ* 1970, 25, pl. 38ϐ. **165:** see **168. 166:** idem, *ΠΑΕ* 1970, 21, pl. 29ϐ; idem, *AAA* 3, 1970, 166, fig. 19. **167:** ibidem fig. 25. **168, 169, 170, 165, 171, 172, 173:** idem, *Έργον* 1970, 12-13; idem, *ΠΑΕ* 1970, 25, 36; idem, *AAA* 3, 1970, fig. 25. **174:** idem, *ΠΑΕ* 1970, 25, pl. 39α; idem *AAA* 3, 1970, fig. 30. **175:** see **162. 176:** idem, *AAA* 3, 1970, fig. 28. **851:** idem, *ΠΑΕ* 1970, 25, pl. 37α; idem, *AAA* 3, 1970, fig. 20.

CASE 12. 205: *ΑΔ* 21, 1966, Β1, 107, pl. 103α. **210:** ibidem pl. 101α-ϐ. **214:** ibidem 107. **230:** ibidem. **234:** Γ. Σωτηριάδης, *ΠΑΕ* 1934, fig. 6. **328:** idem, *ΠΑΕ* 1939, 38, fig. 10. **331:** idem, *ΠΑΕ* 1934, fig. 4. **1482:** Ἑλένη Θεοχαράκη, *ΑΔ* 35, 1980, Β1, 87, pl. 23.

NOTE. An overview of the topography and monuments of Marathon, richly illustrated and with extensive bibliography, is presented in John Travlos, *Bildlexikon zur Topographie des antiken Attika* (Tübingen 1988) 216-221, figs 269-316.

Sources of the photographs

The Archaeological Society at Athens, Drawings Archive: 32. Photographic Archive: 1, 4, 8, 9, 23-25, 30, 31, 33, 35-38, 41, 43, 44, 48-50, 52, 56-82, 84-107.

AΔ: 10. *AJA*: 15b. *AM*: 46. *Ἔργον*: 22. *Hesperia*: 8. Philippe Le Bas, *Voyage archéologique*: 45, 47. *ΠΑΕ*: 16. G.M.A. Richter, *Greek Portraits*: 14. Charles Seltman, *Greek Coins*: 6. John Travlos, *Bildlexikon zur Topographie des antiken Attika*: 7, 17-21, 28, 34, 39, 40, 42.

The Archaeological Society is grateful to the following museums and institutions for kindly granting permission to publish photographs: Acropolis Museum: 15a. Ashmolean Museum: 53. Bibliothèque Nationale de Paris: 26, 27. German Archaeological Institue at Athens: 12, 13 (75/558 and Ol. 4933). German Archaeological Institute at Rome: 3, 11. National Archaeological Museum, Athens: 29, 83. Musée du Louvre, Greek Collection: 54, 55. Staatliche Museen zu Berlin: 2, 51.

The Archaeological Society at Athens

When the state of Greece was founded in 1830, after the War of Independence, the first governments were immediately faced with the great problems of the economy, public administration and education. The last of these also included the question of the country's ancient treasures, which had been looted and destroyed over the centuries by traffickers in antiquities. However, the official Antiquities Service was undermanned and incapable of taking proper care of the ancient remains, and so on 6th January 1837, on the initiative of a wealthy merchant named Konstantinos Belios, a group of scholars and politicians founded *The Archaeological Society at Athens* with the objects of locating, re-erecting and restoring the antiquities of Greece.

The Presidents and Secretaries of the Society in its early days were politicians and diplomats, whose enthusiasm was such that in spite of the shortage of funds —for it was financed entirely by members' subscriptions and voluntary donations and received no assistance whatever from the State— they were able to carry out a number of ambitious projects such as the excavation of the Acropolis, the restoration of the Parthenon and excavations of the Theatre of Dionysos, the Odeion of Herodes Atticus and the Tower of the Winds, all in Athens.

Until 1859 the Society was in such a precarious financial position that it was constantly on the verge of collapse. In that year the distinguished scholar and epigraphist Stephanos Kumanudes became its Secretary, and he held the position until 1894. With his expertise, his methodical mind and his energy he breathed new life into the Society, and on his initiative large-scale excavations were carried out in Athens (the Kerameikos, the Acropolis, Hadrian's Library, the Stoa of Attalos, the Theatre of Dionysos, the Roman Agora), elsewhere in Attica (Rhamnous, Thorikos, Marathon, Eleusis, the Amphiaraeion, Piraeus), and in Boeotia (Chaironeia, Tanagra, Thespiai), the Peloponnese (Mycenae, Epidauros, Lakonia) and the Cyclades. Meanwhile the Society founded several large museums in Athens, which were later amalgamated to form the National Archaeological Museum.

Kumanudes was succeeded by Panayiotis Kavvadias, the General Inspector of Antiquities (1895-1909, 1912-1920), who carried on his predecessor's work with undiminished energy and presided over excavations in other parts of Greece —Thessaly, Epiros, Macedonia and the islands (Euboea, Corfu, Kefallinia, Lesbos, Samos and the Cyclades)— as well as the opening of numerous museums in provincial towns. Kavvadias was succeeded by three university professors, Georgios Oikonomos (1924-1951), Anastasios Orlandos (1951-1979) and Georgios Mylonas (1979-1988). Under them the Society managed to keep up its archaeological activities in spite of the difficulties caused by the Second World War and its aftermath, which hampered its work for a considerable length of time.

As an independent learned society, the Archaeological Society is in a position to assist the State in its work of protecting, improving and studying Greek antiquities. Whenever necessary, it undertakes the management and execution of large projects: this has happened with the excavations in Macedonia and Thrace in recent years and with the large-scale restoration projects in the past.

An important part of the Society's work is its publishing. It brings out three annual titles: *Praktika tes Archaiologikes Hetairias* (*Proceedings of the Archaeological Society*) (since 1837) containing detailed reports on the excavations and researches carried out in all parts of Greece; the *Archaiologike Ephemeris* (since 1837) containing papers on subjects to do with Greek antiquities, including excavation reports; and *Ergon tes Archaiologikes Hetairias* (*The Work of the Archaeological Society*) (since 1955), published every

May, with brief reports on its excavations. *Mentor* is a quarterly whose contents consist mainly of short articles on ancient Greece and the history of Greek archaeology, as well as news of the Society's activities. All these are edited by the Secretary General.

Besides the periodicals, there is the series of books with the general title *The Archaeological Society at Athens Library:* these are monographs on archaeological subjects and reports on excavations, mostly those carried out by the Society.

The Society is administered by an eleven-member Board, elected every three years by the members in General Meeting. Every year, in May or thereabouts, the Secretary General of the Board reports on the Society's activities over the past twelve months at a Public Meeting.

THE BOOK *MARATHON*
BY BASIL PETRAKOS
NO. 155 OF
THE ARCHAEOLOGICAL SOCIETY AT ATHENS LIBRARY
NO. 7 IN THE SERIES
ANCIENT SITES AND MUSEUMS IN GREECE
WAS PRINTED IN 1996
BY 'GRAPHIKES TECHNES
E. BOULOUKOS - A. LOGOTHETIS'
26 MILONOS STREET, ATHENS